This book belongs to

....

....

2025
CHILDREN'S
ALMANAC

Published by Collins
An imprint of
HarperCollins*Publishers*
Westerhill Road
Bishopbriggs
Glasgow
G64 2QT

HarperCollins*Publishers*
Macken House,
39/40 Mayor Street Upper,
Dublin 1, D01 C9W8, Ireland

collins.co.uk

First published 2024

© HarperCollins*Publishers* 2024

Collins® is a registered trademark
of HarperCollins*Publishers* Ltd.

Illustrations by Tania Rex

Text by Stella Caldwell &
          Jennifer Smith

Poems on p.39 & p.127
          © Daniel Thompson

Publisher: Michelle I'Anson
Project leader: Rachel Allegro
Design: James Hunter
Cover: Tania Rex, James Hunter
        & Kevin Robbins
Production: Ilaria Rovera

With thanks to Alexander Allegro

Photo credits
All photos © Shutterstock, except:
pp.19, 23, 27, 43 & 115:
          Rachel Allegro
p.30: Adrian Dennis/Getty
pp.36 (bluebells) & 112:
          Lorraine Inglis
p.69: MI News & Sport
          / Alamy Stock Photo
p.105: Design Pics Inc
          / Alamy Stock Photo

The contents of this publication
are believed correct at the time of
printing. Every care has been taken
in the preparation of this book.
However, the publisher can
accept no responsiblity for errors
or omissions, changes in detail
given or for any expense or
loss thereby caused.

A catalogue record for this book is
available from the British Library.

The publisher and the authors have
made every reasonable effort to
ensure that the activities in this
book are safe when carried out
as instructed but assume no
responsibility for any damage
caused or sustained while
undertaking the activities in this
book to the full extent permitted
by law. This book is intended for
children but parents must ensure
that children engaging in activities
are fully supervised and guided
through the instructions at all times.

WARNING/SAFETY INSTRUCTIONS:
ALWAYS follow all the steps in each
activity carefully. TAKE CARE –
parents may want to take over,
especially when handling hot or
heavy objects, glass, scissors,
knives, matches or other potentially
dangerous materials. ALWAYS read
the safety instructions on any
products and materials used
and ensure that you follow the
manufacturer's guidelines and take
all appropriate safety precautions.

ISBN 9780008686161

Printed by LEGO, Italy.

10 9 8 7 6 5 4 3 2 1

This book contains FSC™ certified
paper and other controlled sources
to ensure responsible forest
management. For more information
visit: www.harpercollins.co.uk/green

2025
CHILDREN'S
ALMANAC

2025

January

February

May

June

September

October

WELCOME TO 2025!

This almanac contains lots of information about what is happening each month throughout 2025. Every month is packed full of information, activities and ideas that will inspire you to explore what's going on in nature, gaze into the night sky, get stuck in with sports, experiment with science and learn about different cultures around the world.

What is an almanac?

An almanac is a book that records important information about a given year. The first almanac to be printed was in Europe in 1457, but almanacs – in different forms – were around way before then.

Ancient Greeks used almanacs as a way to track patterns in the weather over a year, so that they could predict when to plant seeds and harvest their crops. Astronomers from the same period of time also found almanacs very useful for predicting Moon phases and recording patterns in the stars.

Today, almanacs are still used in a similar way by farmers and stargazers, but almanacs like this one help you make the most of your year, by providing you with interesting facts and exciting activities to keep you entertained the whole year round!

You'll find a calendar for each month which includes some of the world's festivals, holidays and special days, plus there's space to record events that are important to you.

Do events happen at the same time every year?

Yes and no! Some events happen on a certain day every single year without fail, for example, Christmas.

Other events, like Eid in the Islamic calendar, are linked to the Moon, so change dates each year.

The dates of sports events can also change because of circumstances out of human control, such as extreme weather.

Take care!

Throughout this almanac, you'll find lots of ideas for activities, crafts and recipes. When carrying out activities that use sharp tools, like knives or scissors, always ask a grown-up to help you. Some of the outdoor activities involve being around water, or going outside at night to stargaze. Only do these activities if you have a grown-up with you.

January

MONDAY	TUESDAY	WEDNESDAY	THURSDAY
		1 New Year's Day	2
6	7	8	9
13	14	15	16
20 National Cheese Lovers' Day	21	22	23
27	28	29 Chinese New Year	30

Why not add your own special days to the calendar?

FRIDAY	SATURDAY	SUNDAY
3	4 World Braille Day	5
10	11	12
17	18 Winnie the Pooh™ Day	19 World Religion Day
24 International Day of Education	25 Burns Night	26 International Day of Clean Energy
31 International Zebra Day		

HAPPY NEW YEAR!

In most parts of the world, the first day of January marks the start of a new year. It's a time of celebration, and to think about your hopes and dreams for the year ahead.

The start of a new year has been celebrated for thousands of years – but not always on 1 January. In ancient Babylonia, the new year began when the crops began to grow in mid-March. The ancient Egyptians celebrated the start of a new year when the Nile River flooded its banks in late summer.

In 1582, Pope Gregory XIII introduced the Gregorian Calendar, with 1 January as New Year's Day. This is the calendar that most countries follow today.

New Year celebrations begin on the last night of December, New Year's Eve. Different countries have their own traditions.

In Spain, 12 grapes are eaten at midnight, representing each stroke of the clock.

In New York, USA, people gather to watch the famous Times Square ball drop.

At the start of a new year, it's traditional to make New Year's resolutions – goals for the year ahead. Use these ideas to write your own resolutions.

* Somewhere I'd like to go
* A new skill I'd like to learn
* Something I want to do better
* A good deed I'd like to do

MAKE A
TIME CAPSULE

Time capsules are a great way to celebrate the year that's just ended. Open your capsule when you're older and travel back in time!

You'll need

- An empty box, e.g. a shoe box
- Wrapping paper, paint, stickers, things to decorate it

What to do

1. Decorate the box and its lid. You could wrap it in colourful paper, paint it, or cover it with photos.

2. Put the date on the box.

3. Think about what to include in your time capsule to sum up the past year. Here are some ideas...

   * An 'All About Me' page, e.g. your height, best friend, pets, hobbies...
   * A drawing or painting
   * Photos and mementos, e.g. a cinema ticket
   * Fashion pages from a magazine
   * A letter to your future self

4. Place the items in the box and seal it with tape. Hide it somewhere dry in your house, to be opened in the future!

GARDEN BIRDS

January is often the coldest month of the year. It can be a struggle for birds to keep warm and find enough food to survive.

Winter gardens are full of birds looking for something to eat:

Blackbird

Blackbirds forage on the ground for grubs and berries.

Blue tit

Blue tits look for insects and berries in hedges and trees.

Robin

Robins chase away bigger birds to get enough to eat!

Starling

Noisy starlings feed together in groups.

Growing bird-friendly plants is a great way to help birds over the winter months. Evergreen trees and shrubs provide shelter from rain and snow, while winter berries make tasty snacks.

Hawthorn

Ivy

Rosehip

Holly

MAKE A BIRD FEEDER

Set up a bird cafe by making this simple feeder. It's a great way to attract different species to your outdoor space, and it will be fun to see which neighbourhood birds pay a visit! You can also scatter kitchen scraps, such as fruit, cheese and cooked rice, on the ground. Make sure there is always clean drinking water too. Place a water dish in a sunny spot to stop it freezing on cold days.

You'll need

- Cardboard tube, such as kitchen or toilet roll
- Scissors
- Butter knife
- String
- Thin stick
- Lard or suet
- Bird seed, on a plate

What to do

1. Cut two holes near the bottom of the tube for the stick. Make sure the holes aren't too big, or the stick will slip out.

2. Cut two small holes near the top of the tube for the string.

3. Use the knife to spread lard or suet over the tube.

4. Roll the tube in bird seed until it's completely covered.

5. Thread the stick through the bottom holes to form a perch. Then thread the string through the holes at the top.

6. Hang the feeder from a tree or washing line. Keep it away from thick foliage, where a cat could hide!

QUADRANTIDS METEOR SHOWER

The Quadrantids meteor shower appears in early January – and the good news is, you won't need any special equipment to watch it.

Have you ever wished on a shooting star? What you're seeing is a meteor – a small piece of space rock that has entered Earth's atmosphere at incredible speed. This causes it to heat up and glow brightly as it streaks across the sky.

A meteor shower happens when Earth passes through the trail of dust and debris left by a comet or asteroid. During a meteor shower, many meteors appear to come from the same part of the sky.

Meteor showers are named after the constellation of stars from which they seem to come. The Quadrantids was named after an old constellation called 'Quadrans Muralis'. This group of stars is now part of the large constellations Boötes, Draco and Hercules.

Quadrantids meteor shower

The Quadrantids will appear to come from the constellation Boötes, near the famous star pattern called the Plough or the Big Dipper. This pattern is made up of four bright stars forming a bowl, and three bright stars in the shape of a handle.

Follow the line of the Plough's handle to the orange star Arcturus. This is the brightest star in Boötes.

JANUARY MOON PHASES

6th   13th   21st   29th

Look up at the sky and notice the changing shape of the Moon over the month!

SPOT THE QUADRANTIDS

In 2025, the best time to see the Quadrantids will be on the evening of 2 January until the early hours of 3 January. Here are some top tips for a great view of it...

* Check the weather forecast, and make sure you are dressed for the conditions. Warm clothing is essential — you may be outside for some time!

* It's best to view meteor showers in a quiet place, away from city lights. Ask a grown-up to help you choose somewhere suitable and to go with you.

* Take something to make you comfortable, such as a blanket, and a flask with a hot drink and some snacks too.

* Once you're settled, let your eyes get used to the dark. When they're adapted, sit back and look at the sky!

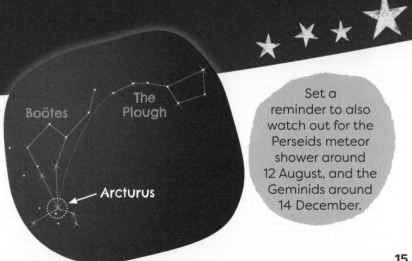

Boötes

The Plough

Arcturus

Set a reminder to also watch out for the Perseids meteor shower around 12 August, and the Geminids around 14 December.

INTERNATIONAL DAY OF CLEAN ENERGY

Humans use a lot of energy – it's needed to light houses, drive cars and fly to faraway places. Have you ever wondered where this power comes from?

Today, much of the world's energy comes from burning fossil fuels, such as oil and coal. This process releases gases, which cause pollution and lead to global warming. This is a major cause of climate change.

'Clean energy' is important for the planet because it comes from a natural source, like the wind or the sun, and causes less harm to the environment. It is often called 'renewable energy', because unlike oil or coal, the source will never run out.

Lots of countries are trying to change the way they produce energy, but there's still a lot of work to be done.

Wind turbines' spinning blades produce electricity from wind power.

Solar panels soak up the sun's rays to create electricity.

Water from dams and rivers spins turbines to create 'hydroelectricity'.

The International Day of Clean Energy is on 26 January. It calls for Earth's resources to be used wisely. Switching from fossil fuels to clean energy will mean that future generations can continue to enjoy our beautiful planet.

MAKE A PINWHEEL

This activity will show you how a wind turbine uses wind power to create energy. The 'blades' act like cups. When you hold the pinwheel in the wind or blow on it, the cups capture the moving air, making the blades spin.

You'll need

- Square piece of paper
- Scissors
- Pencil
- Ruler
- Paper straw
- Pushpin
- Masking tape

> You can use any paper – plain, patterned, thick or thin. Regular paper is easier to fold; thick paper makes a sturdier pinwheel.

What to do

1. Using the ruler and pencil, draw a dot at the centre of the paper. Next draw four diagonal lines from each corner, stopping around 2 cm from the dot.

2. Use the scissors to cut down the diagonal lines.

3. Bring the right-hand corner (or the left-hand corner) of each triangle to the central dot and pin them in place with the pushpin.

4. Holding the pushpin and folded paper in one hand, use your other hand to push the end of the pin through the straw. Cover the sharp end with masking tape.

5. Take your pinwheel outside and test it in the wind. If there's no wind, see how much wind power you can create by blowing on it!

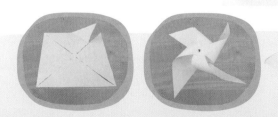

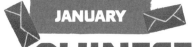

CHINESE NEW YEAR

Chinese New Year is celebrated around the world. It is also called the Spring Festival or Lunar New Year.

The starting date for Chinese New Year changes each year. The festival begins with the New Moon in late January or February and lasts 15 days until the Full Moon. In 2025, it will begin on 29 January.

Many legends surround Chinese New Year. One story tells of how a fierce monster called Nian attacked people when a new year started. The only things that could scare it away were bright lights, loud noises and the colour red. That is why these things are an important part of celebrations today!

People prepare for the new year by cleaning their homes – a sign of sweeping away bad luck. Houses and streets are decorated with red lanterns and other decorations. On Chinese New Year's Eve, families gather to eat a special meal. Children often receive gifts of money in red envelopes.

In China, dragons are a symbol of good luck. Many areas hold a dragon dance, where a dragon model is paraded through the streets.

Did you know?

In Chinese culture, each year is connected to one of the 12 animals of the Chinese Zodiac. 2025 is the year of the snake. Children born in this year are said to be smart and quick-thinking!

MAKE A PAPER SNAKE

Make lots of cute, short paper snakes, or a super-long one to stretch all the way around a room.

You'll need

- Coloured paper (two colours work well)
- Scissors
- Glue
- Pencil
- Black felt tip pen, or marker pen

What to do

1. Cut a sheet of paper into strips lengthwise, about 2.5 cm across. If you're using a sheet of A4 paper, it's easiest to fold the paper in half three times until you have 8 strips. Then cut along the folds.

2. Place two strips on a table at a right angle (90°) to each other and glue the ends together. Fold the bottom strip (a) over the top strip (b), keeping the right angle. Continue folding the bottom strip over the top one until you reach the strip ends.

3. Glue another two strips to the ends and continue folding. Keep going until you're happy with the length of your snake.

4. Draw a snake's head on some paper and cut it out. Then draw and cut out the shape of a snake's forked tongue.

5. Draw on some eyes and nostrils.

6. Glue the snake's tongue under the head, and then glue the head to the snake's body.

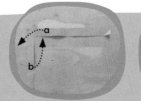

February

MONDAY	TUESDAY	WEDNESDAY	THURSDAY
3	4	5	6
10	11 International Day of Women and Girls in Science	12	13 World Radio Day
17 Random Acts of Kindness Day	18	19	20
24	25	26	27 International Polar Bear Day

FRIDAY	SATURDAY	SUNDAY
	1	2 Yorkshire Pudding Day
7	8	9
14 ♥ Valentine's Day	15 World Hippo Day	16 World Whale Day
21 International Mother Language Day	22 World Thinking Day	23
28		

WINTER WEATHER

Winter brings long, dark nights and icy winds. It is the coldest season of the year, but there are still plenty of things to enjoy about winter weather!

Winter is caused by Earth's changing position as it moves around the Sun. When one side, or hemisphere, is pointed away from the Sun, it receives less sunlight. The days become shorter and temperatures fall.

In the Northern Hemisphere, the winter months are December, January and February. In the Southern Hemisphere, winter is in June, July and August.

Did you know?

The word 'winter' comes from an old German word, 'wintar', meaning 'wet'. In the Northern Hemisphere, winter brings rain, ice and snow.

When it's very cold, moisture in the air freezes and covers the ground and plants with an icy layer of frost. Sometimes, you can see beautiful patterns in frost crystals.

Clouds that give us rain can produce snow in the winter. Water freezes in the clouds and forms ice crystals. These fall to the ground as snowflakes. All snowflakes have six sides, but no two look the same!

When snowflakes start to melt on their way down, they fall as sleet – a wet mixture of rain and snow.

ICE ART

Create magical ice ornaments and hang them on branches where they will shimmer like crystals in the sunlight!

You'll need

- Small bowls or a cupcake tray
- Kettle to boil water
- String or wool
- Scissors
- Natural items e.g. leaves, bright berries, small pinecones, feathers or sliced fruit

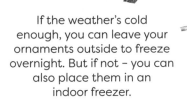

If the weather's cold enough, you can leave your ornaments outside to freeze overnight. But if not – you can also place them in an indoor freezer.

What to do

1. Boil some water. This helps the water to freeze without air bubbles.

2. Put the bowls or cupcake tray on a flat surface. Arrange your natural items in these containers.

3. Place a long piece of string or wool in each container – make sure you leave enough hanging over the edge to tie the ornament from a branch.

4. Once the water has cooled, pour it into the containers.

5. Put the containers outside on a cold night.

6. Once the water has frozen, put the containers in a basin of cold water to separate them from the ice, and then hang the decorations outside.

WOMEN AND GIRLS IN SCIENCE

11 February is International Day of Women and Girls in Science. The date celebrates trailblazing women and girls who have made great advances in science, such as Marie Curie.

Marie Curie was born in Poland, in 1867. It was a time when women had few opportunities to study, but she didn't let this hold her back! Her important work led to radiation being used as a treatment for diseases such as cancer, and to the development of X-rays. She was the first woman to win the Nobel Prize, and the only person to win the Nobel Prize in more than one science.

Throughout history, many women have made ground-breaking scientific discoveries, though their contributions haven't always been celebrated. Here are a few of them...

* Ada Lovelace wrote the first computer code.
* Mary Anning discovered many fossils, including the world's first plesiosaur.
* Rosalind Franklin's work led to the discovery of the structure of DNA — the code in our bodies that makes us who we are.

Today, girls and women have more opportunities to study science, but less than 30% of the world's scientists are female. International Day of Women and Girls in Science aims to inspire more women and girls to make their mark.

KIARA NIRGHIN

At the age of just sixteen, South African inventor Kiara Nirghin won a Google Science Fair award with a project called 'No More Thirsty Crops'.

In 2015, South Africa was hit by a severe drought. The lack of rain had a terrible effect on farmers and communities.

Kiara was directly affected by the drought when it caused her to develop a disease called bilharzia. She spent a year in hospital and could not go to school. Although she was in a lot of pain, she used this time to start thinking about a solution to drought.

During her recovery, Kiara's research led her to invent a material made from orange peel and the skin of avocados that can be planted in soil. It can hold 300 times its weight in rainfall, and slowly releases water into dry soil. The exciting thing about this invention is that it is cheap to make and is also environmentally friendly.

Since winning her science award, Kiara has begun studying computer science. She often gives talks, hoping to inspire girls to study science and technology.

Perhaps you are a future scientist? What will you study and where will you go?

VALENTINE'S DAY

Valentine's Day, celebrated on 14 February, is all about spreading love! Many people around the world exchange cards with affectionate messages.

This special day gets its name from Saint Valentine – though nobody is sure who he was! In one popular story, he was a Roman priest. At the time, marriage was banned because single men were thought to make better soldiers. Valentine thought this was unfair and secretly married young couples.

Valentine was caught breaking the rules and was imprisoned. In jail, he fell in love with the jailer's daughter and was sentenced to death. On 14 February, he wrote a farewell letter to his beloved. It was signed, 'From your Valentine'.

Today, Valentine's cards are often decorated with red hearts, and it is popular to give gifts such as chocolates or a bouquet of red roses.

RANDOM ACTS OF KINDNESS DAY

This day is celebrated three days after Valentine's Day, on 17 February. Why don't you surprise someone by doing something kind? You could help a friend, offer to make dinner or give someone a compliment. It feels good to spread kindness!

THUMBPRINT HEART COOKIES

You'll need

- Baking sheet
- Baking paper
- 170 g butter*
- 100 g soft brown sugar
- 1 egg*

- ½ teaspoon vanilla extract
- 250 g plain flour
- ¼ teaspoon salt
- 80 g jam

*To make vegan cookies, use vegan spread instead of butter, and 1 tablespoon of flaxseed mixed with 2 tablespoons of water instead of an egg.

What to do

1. Preheat the oven to 190°C and line a baking sheet with baking paper.

2. Use an electric mixer or a spoon to mix together the butter and sugar until fluffy. Add the egg and vanilla extract and mix. Then add the flour and salt, mixing until all the ingredients are combined.

3. Shape the dough into balls, about 2½ cm across. Place them on the baking sheet, about 4 cm apart. Press your thumb or the back of a teaspoon into each centre twice, to form a heart shape. This is where the jam will go.

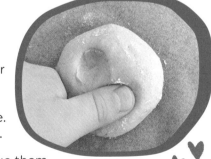

4. Ask an adult to help you bake them for 12–15 minutes, until golden. Remove from the oven and transfer to a cooling rack.

5. Once the cookies have cooled, fill the centres with jam.

WORLD HIPPO DAY

Every year, World Hippo Day falls on 15 February. The marvellous, mud-loving hippopotamus was once found throughout Africa, but today this creature is under threat.

Hippos are mainly found in East Africa. These hefty mammals spend most of their time in rivers or lakes to protect their skin from the hot sun. A hippo's eyes and nostrils are near the top of its head so it can see and breathe while wallowing in water.

Hippos live in groups of around 20 individuals. The group is led by a powerful male who warns rivals away with fierce grunts and loud splashing. Female hippos give birth to a calf every two years. Each night, hippos come out of the water to search for food. They mainly munch grass – and lots of it!

They may look like gentle giants but hippos are one of the world's most dangerous land mammals. Their enormous mouths and long teeth can deliver a ferocious bite.

Hippos are hunted for their meat and ivory teeth, and farming is destroying the places where they live. World Hippo Day reminds us that more needs to be done to protect these wonderful creatures.

Did you know?
Although hippos love water, they can't swim! In deep water, they walk or run along the river bed. They can hold their breath for up to five minutes and push themselves up to the surface to breathe.

DRAW A HIPPO

Anyone can draw a hippo if you follow these simple instructions. Use a pencil to lightly draw the shapes, and then rub out the lines you don't need once you're finished. Why not make a card for someone to wish them Happy Hippo Day!

❶
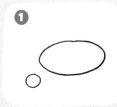

Draw an oval shape for the hippo's body, and a small circle for the bottom of its head.

❷

Draw lines for the hippo's head and bottom.

❸

Add lines for the legs.

❹

Rub out the lines you don't need and add detail to form the snout and nostrils. Add more lines for the legs and tail.

❺
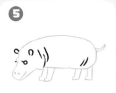

Draw the hippo's ears, eyes and skin creases.

❻
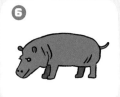

Shade or colour your hippo.

zzz...

ICC CHAMPIONS TROPHY

The top cricketing nations will compete against each other in the 2025 ICC Champions Trophy. This action-packed tournament is watched by millions of cricket fans all around the world.

Pakistan won the last ICC Champions Trophy, held in 2017. They are the defending champions, and they defeated the favourites, India, in a thrilling final.

The ICC Champions Trophy is like a mini Cricket World Cup – but while the World Cup can last for more than six weeks, this tournament lasts around two weeks. It is expected to start in February.

The sides are split into two groups. Each team plays the others in their group once, with the top two sides in each group reaching the semi-finals.

The matches are played in the One Day International (ODI) format. That means each team gets to bat for up to 50 overs while the other team bowls (in cricket, an over consists of six balls bowled).

This will be the ninth tournament since the competition began, in 1998. The first two tournaments were called the ICC KnockOuts – there were no groups, and in each game, the losing side was knocked out of the competition.

GAME ON!

Watching the 2025 ICC Champions Trophy will be a lot more enjoyable if you know a little about the history of the tournament. Brush up on these fun facts and stats, and wow your family and friends with your in-depth knowledge!

First country to lift the title
South Africa, 1998

Most games won
India have won 18 of their 27 games.

Most centuries scored
India, with 10 centuries

Most catches
Sri Lankan batsman, Mahela Jayawardene, took 15 catches in 22 matches.

First player to score a century
Alistair Campbell of Zimbabwe, in 1998

Most wickets
Kyle Mills of New Zealand, took 28 wickets in 15 matches.

Biggest number of tournament victories
Australia (2006, 2009) and India (2002, 2013)

March

MONDAY	TUESDAY	WEDNESDAY	THURSDAY
3 World Wildlife Day	4	5	6 World Book Day
10	11	12	13
17	18 Global Recycling Day	19	20 International Day of Happiness
24	25	26	27
31			

FRIDAY	SATURDAY	SUNDAY
	1	2
7	8 International Women's Day	9
14 Partial lunar eclipse	15	16
21 International Day of Forests	22 World Water Day	23
28	29 Partial solar eclipse	30 Mother's Day Eid al-Fitr*

*Dates may vary slightly by location.

SPRING WILDFLOWERS

After the dark, cold winter, March brings the first signs of spring. The days are longer and warmer, birdsong fills the air and wildflowers begin to bloom.

Woodlands are a great place to see wildflowers, but you can also spot them along rivers and roadsides, beneath hedgerows and in open fields and parks.

Wildflowers aren't just beautiful to look at. They also provide food for pollinating insects, such as bees and butterflies. These insects help flowers, fruits and vegetables to grow by carrying pollen from plant to plant.

Lesser celandine is one of the earliest wildflowers to bloom.

Golden daffodils provide a blanket of colour.

Blackthorn trees produce clouds of white blossom.

Star-shaped wood anemones slowly spread across woodlands.

Sometimes wildflowers need our help – as towns and cities get bigger, it's not always easy for them to find space to grow. You can help by planting wildflower seeds in your garden, in outdoor plant pots or in window boxes. You could also ask your school to set aside a space where pupils can create a wildflower garden.

MAKE WILDFLOWER SEED BALLS

Create your own mini meadow by making these wildflower seed balls and launching them into your outdoor space. Early spring (March and April) are the best months to plant wildflower seeds, or early autumn (September).

The flowers that pop up will create a beautiful splash of colour, and you'll be helping bees and butterflies to do their important work.

You'll need

- Native wildflower seeds
- Bucket or bowl for mixing
- Tray or large plate
- Peat-free compost
- Flour
- Water

What to do

1. Mix 10 parts of compost to 2 parts of flour. Slowly add water, until you have a sticky dough.

2. Shape the dough into balls the size of golf balls.

3. Place the seeds on the tray or plate.

4. Roll the balls in the seeds until they're evenly covered.

5. Leave the seed balls in a dry spot for 24 hours.

6. Throw the balls into an empty part of your garden and let nature do its work! Check with an adult that it's OK to do so first.

WORLD WILDLIFE DAY

World Wildlife Day takes place on 3 March. It celebrates the brilliant animals and plants found on Earth and reminds us to take care of them.

Hedgehogs are disappearing from gardens and countryside.

The woodland bluebell is a protected plant.

The small tortoiseshell butterfly is no longer a common garden visitor.

Water voles are harmed by water pollution.

One of the best ways to support wildlife is to help the creatures that visit your outdoor space. You could put out a bird or butterfly feeder, build a hedgehog house or make a mini pond.

Small changes in your behaviour can also have a big impact. Recycling paper helps to save trees, and picking up litter stops wild animals from eating things that might harm them.

MAKE A MINI POND

A pond is a wonderful way to attract wildlife to your outdoor space. Make sure you provide stepping stones so that if an animal falls into the water, it can get out again!

You'll need

- A watertight container, e.g. a washing-up bowl
- Small stones or gravel
- Stones, sticks and twigs
- Small trowel (if you want to dig the container into soil)
- Pond plants (optional)

What to do

1. Choose a suitable spot outside, with a mixture of light and shade. Dig the container into the soil, making the top level with the soil so that wildlife can get in and out.

2. Put some gravel or small stones in the bottom.

3. Place larger stones and twigs on top of the gravel in the container to create stepping stones and ladders.

4. Fill the pond with rain water.

5. Add pond plants if you have them.

6. Place flat stones or sticks around the container edges.

If you use tap water to fill your pond, leave it to stand somewhere for 24 hours before pouring it into the pond, to get rid of chemicals.

INTERNATIONAL DAY OF HAPPINESS

This special day is celebrated on 20 March. It reminds you to be grateful for the things that make you happy, and to spread a little kindness and joy to the people around you.

It's okay to feel sad sometimes. You can't always control what happens to you, but you *can* decide how to respond. See if these ideas help improve your mood.

1. Share your worries. Talking to a trusted adult can help you to find solutions, and to see things differently.

2. Deep breathing helps you to feel calm and relaxed. Try doing this exercise for a few minutes, regularly...

* Find somewhere quiet to lie on your back. Close your eyes and place your hands on your belly.
* Slowly breathe in through your nose until your lungs feel full.
* Hold your breath for a few seconds.
* Slowly breathe out through your mouth.

3. Do something that makes you feel happy. Go for a walk, watch a favourite film or bake a cake. It's important to do the things you love!

4. Make a gratitude jar. On a piece of paper, write down something you're grateful for and place it in an empty jar. Add something to your jar every day – it will help you to have positive thoughts, especially if you read them back.

5. Make positive pebbles! Turn stones into positive works of art by decorating them. Keep them nearby as a reminder to think happy thoughts or give them away as encouraging gifts.

Leave Worries Behind

By Daniel Thompson

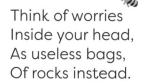

Think of worries
Inside your head,
As useless bags,
Of rocks instead.

They may be yours,
But have no doubt.
They'll weigh you down,
And wear you out.

So let them go!
Leave them behind!
It's odd at first,
But soon you'll find.

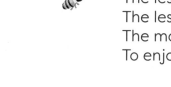

The less you carry,
The less you weigh.
The more you're free,
To enjoy your day.

ECLIPSES

An eclipse is when a planet or a moon gets in the way of the Sun's light. Here on Earth, we experience solar eclipses and lunar eclipses. In March 2025, we will have the chance to see both!

Lunar eclipse

A lunar eclipse happens when the Earth is between the Sun and the Moon. The Earth casts a shadow over the Moon, which often has a reddish tint.

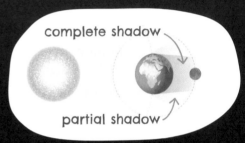

complete shadow

partial shadow

On 14 March 2025, a partial lunar eclipse will be visible in the UK in the early hours of the morning. Unlike a solar eclipse, it's safe to look at a lunar eclipse. You just need a clear sky!

Solar eclipse

A solar eclipse happens when the Moon passes between the Earth and the Sun, blocking the Sun's light. If the Moon, Earth and Sun are in a straight line, Earth's sky falls dark. This is known as a total eclipse.

In a partial solar eclipse, the Moon is not exactly between the Sun and the Earth, and only a part of the Sun is blotted out. A partial solar eclipse will be visible in the UK on 29 March 2025.

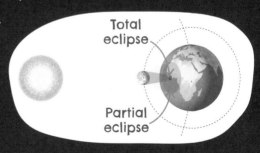

Total eclipse

Partial eclipse

MARCH MOON PHASES

 6th 14th 22nd 29th

VIEW THE PARTIAL SOLAR ECLIPSE

Watching a solar eclipse is an amazing experience, but you should never look at the Sun without proper eye protection. It could damage your eyesight or even cause blindness.

Safety first!

* Never look directly at the Sun, even for a second.
* Don't look at the Sun through sunglasses.
* Don't look at the Sun through a smartphone, camera, binoculars or a telescope.

You can buy solar eclipse glasses to view the Sun safely. Make sure the glasses are safe, and not damaged or scratched.

MAKE A PINHOLE CAMERA

One of the best ways to watch a solar eclipse is to make a pinhole camera. It's cheap and easy – and completely safe! All you need is two pieces of card and a pair of scissors.

What to do

1. Cut a hole in the centre of one of the pieces of card, around 4 mm across.

2. Place the second piece of card on the ground.

3. With your back to the Sun, hold the card with the hole above the piece of card on the floor to project an image of the Sun onto it. The pieces of card should be at least 1 metre apart.

EID AL-FITR

Each year, Muslims around the world celebrate Eid al-Fitr, which marks the end of Ramadan.

During the month of Ramadan, many Muslims fast from sunrise to sunset, which means they don't eat or drink anything during daylight hours. It's a time for drawing closer to Allah, or God.

The date for Eid changes each year because the Islamic calendar is based on the cycles of the Moon. The end of Ramadan is marked by the sighting of the New Moon. In 2025, that date is expected to be 30 March, but this date could change if the New Moon isn't seen.

Eid is a time to share food with family and friends, to give to charity and to exchange gifts. Sweet treats are an important part of the celebrations.

Eid Mubarak

On the morning of Eid, many Muslims go to their mosque to pray. It's traditional to wear new clothes and to greet people by saying 'Eid Mubarak', which means 'Blessed Eid'.

Eid means 'festival' or 'feast' in Arabic. Eid al-Fitr means 'the feast of breaking the fast'.

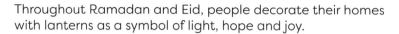

MAKE AN EID LANTERN

Throughout Ramadan and Eid, people decorate their homes with lanterns as a symbol of light, hope and joy.

You'll need

- Scissors
- A4 paper or card
- Ruler
- Paint and paintbrush, or coloured pens/pencils
- Glue or sticky tape

What to do

1. Use a ruler to draw a line 3 cm from the shorter edge of the paper/card. Cut off the strip to become the handle.

2. With the longest edge closest to you, fold the remaining paper in half from bottom to top.

3. Draw a line 3 cm from one edge of the paper. The line should start at the fold and finish 3 cm from the top.

4. Continue drawing lines every 3–4 cm along the fold. Don't worry if the last strip isn't the same width as the others.

5. Unfold your paper and draw/paint a design on the side with the lines. Moon and star shapes are a popular theme for Eid.

6. Refold the paper. Cut along the guidelines from the fold – but be careful not to cut all the way to the top!

7. Unfold the paper and glue or tape the shorter ends together to form a cylinder.

8. Attach the handle from Step 1 with glue or tape.

April

MONDAY	TUESDAY	WEDNESDAY	THURSDAY
	1 April Fool's Day	2	3
7 International Beaver Day	8	9	10
14 World Quantum Day Vaisakhi	15 World Art Day	16	17
21	22 Earth Day	23	24
28	29 International Dance Day	30 International Guide Dog Day	

FRIDAY	SATURDAY	SUNDAY
4	5 International Pillow Fight Day	6
11	12	13
18	19	20 Easter Sunday
25 World Penguin Day	26	27 London Marathon

45

GROW YOUR OWN

There is something special about watching seeds growing into tasty things to eat! April brings sunshine and showers, which makes it the perfect month for planting vegetables and fruit.

You don't need a vegetable patch – you can also grow crops in outdoor pots and containers filled with compost. Your pot or container should be at least 30 cm across and have drainage holes.

Choose an outdoor spot with plenty of sun, and make sure you water your plants regularly...

* Plant carrot seeds 1 cm deep and 7 cm apart. Seedlings will pop up within a few weeks.
* Earthy beetroots are packed full of goodness. Sow the seeds in the ground or a pot about 2 cm deep and 10 cm apart.
* Peppery rocket makes a great salad and grows quickly! Scatter the seeds thinly, about 1 cm deep.
* Crops such as tomatoes and courgettes should be grown inside until the weather is warmer.

Did you know?

1 April is April Fool's Day. Put some googly eyes on fruit so when someone has a snack, it will be looking right back at them!

GROW YOUR OWN STRAWBERRIES

Juicy strawberries are one of summer's tastiest treats. These delicious fruits are bursting with vitamin C and are easy to grow. Plant them in pots, window boxes, hanging baskets or even an old pair of wellies! Find a sunny spot for them and remember to water them every day.

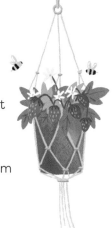

You'll need

- Strawberry plants
- Multi-purpose compost
- Tomato feed
- Stones or gravel
- A container with drainage holes (if you use wellies, cut holes in the soles)

Strawberries make a tasty treat for birds too, so it's a good idea to cover the fruits with a net when they appear!

What to do

1. Put a layer of stones or gravel in the bottom of your container. This helps extra water to drain away.

2. Fill the container with compost.

3. Plant the strawberry plants so that their roots are just buried, 10–20 cm apart.

4. Water your plants daily. Once the flowers have bloomed, use tomato feed once a week to help them grow bigger and stronger.

Pumpkins might make you think of autumn, but April is the best time to plant them. Sow seeds in empty yogurt pots filled with compost and keep them inside on a sunny windowsill. Then, when it's a little warmer in May, plant the seedlings outdoors. Make sure you give your pumpkins enough space to grow!

Pumpkins

WORLD QUANTUM DAY

Everything around you is made up of quantum stuff! World Quantum Day, celebrated on 14 April, raises awareness about this mind-boggling science.

Have you heard of atoms? Imagine them as tiny model bricks that are the building blocks of everything. Water, air and even our own bodies are made up of atoms.

Scientists once thought that atoms were the smallest things in the Universe, but we now know that they are made up of even smaller things, called particles. Quantum physics is the study of these tiny particles.

In the world of quantum physics, things don't behave as you might expect. A particle might be in two places at the same time or spin in different directions at once. This can be difficult even for brilliant scientists to understand!

Did you know?
World Quantum Day was created to spark interest in quantum physics and to show people how it's changing the world. The science is already at work in many amazing technologies used today.

Can you think of any ways that quantum physics has had an impact on your everyday life? What about these?

* Gadgets like smartphones work better and faster thanks to quantum physics.

* MRI machines, which allow doctors to take detailed pictures inside our bodies, rely on this science.

* Quantum computers are being used to develop new medicines.

SATELLITES

Satellites that orbit Earth are able to keep accurate time because of quantum technology.

There are thousands of artificial satellites in space, and they have lots of different uses. Some allow humans back on Earth to communicate, while others help produce weather forecasts.

Satellites have to be able to produce their own power, so most are fitted with solar arrays – collections of solar panels – which help them produce power to operate while in orbit.

The most famous satellite is the International Space Station (ISS). Astronauts live inside this big satellite so that they can study space, and learn more about what it's like to live and work there. The ISS travels at 28,000 km/h, which means that it orbits Earth once every 90 minutes. Because of this, astronauts in the ISS can see up to 16 sunrises within 24 hours!

International Space Station

Can you spot the ISS in the night sky?

LOOK AT THE NIGHT SKY

The Lyrid meteor shower is best seen between 22 and 23 April, and is known to display very bright meteors, called fireballs. The Moon will be a crescent, rising in the morning shortly before sunrise. This is good for spotting meteors because it means the sky will be darker. The meteors will appear to come from the constellation Lyra, the lyre – an instrument a bit like a harp.

APRIL
MOON
PHASES

 5th   13th   21st   27th

VAISAKHI

Vaisakhi is one of the most important Sikh festivals of the year. It celebrates the founding of the Sikh community, called the Khalsa, in 1699.

The story of Vaisakhi and the Khalsa

Vaisakhi used to be known as the harvest festival in Punjab – a region in the north of India. In 1699, Sikhs gathered to celebrate the harvest, and the tenth guru (mentor), Guru Gobind Singh Ji, asked if anyone was willing to give their life to Sikhism.

A man volunteered himself and followed Guru Gobind Singh Ji into a tent. Guru Gobind Singh Ji came out of the tent on his own, carrying his sword. He asked if anyone else was prepared to give their life to their religion, and the same thing happened until five men had gone into the tent.

The men, however, had not died. They emerged from the tent alive and wearing turbans. From that moment, they became known as the 'Panj Pyare', which means the 'Beloved Five'. These five men became the first members of the Khalsa – the baptised Sikh community. Today, many Sikhs choose to be baptised into the Khalsa on Vaisakhi.

CELEBRATIONS

Every year, Sikhs around the world celebrate Vaisakhi on either 13 or 14 April. In 2025, it will be celebrated on 14 April.

On the morning of Vaisakhi, it is traditional to gather at a Gurdwara – the Sikh place of worship – for a special service. Gurdwaras are decorated with bright colours and flowers.

Vaisakhi celebrations also include lots of processions through the streets which are cleaned and cleared by volunteers called sevadaars. These processions – called 'Nagar Kirtans' – involve lots of singing, chanting and dancing, and end with a prayer called 'ardaas'. People wear bright colours.

Langar at a Gurdwara

Food for everyone

After the service, a free meal – known as 'langar' – is often eaten at the Gurdwara. People come together to share this meal, regardless of who they are or their race or religion. This shows the importance of equality, sharing and caring for others in the Sikh faith. The meal that is served is always vegetarian so that people with different beliefs can take part.

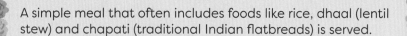

A simple meal that often includes foods like rice, dhaal (lentil stew) and chapati (traditional Indian flatbreads) is served.

LONDON MARATHON

Every year, thousands of runners take part in the famous London Marathon – a running race of 26.2 miles (42.195 km). The event is much more than a long-distance race, though – it's the biggest fundraising event on the planet!

In 2025, the marathon takes place on 27 April. The event was first held in 1981, with 6,255 runners crossing the finishing line.

Runners of all abilities take part, from top athletes to people who run for fun. The event also includes and supports people with disabilities. Elite wheelchair athletes from around the world compete in the wheelchair marathon race.

The London marathon raises a huge amount of money for charity. Many runners dress in weird and wonderful costumes, from a Big Ben outfit to a rhino suit.

In 2002, Lloyd Scott took more than six days to complete the London Marathon because he was wearing a heavy deep-sea diving suit from the 1940s.

Did you know?

The London Marathon begins in Greenwich Park and finishes in front of Buckingham Palace, on the Mall. During the race, competitors get a look at some of the city's well-known sights.

Follow the Route!

Mile 6: The *Cutty Sark* was built in 1869 to carry tea from China to England. It was one of the fastest ships of its time!

Mile 12: Tower Bridge, with its castle-like towers, is one of London's most recognised sights.

Mile 21: Rainbow Row, normally called Butcher's Row, is turned into a colourful street carnival for the marathon.

Mile 25: The London Eye, on the banks of the Thames, is one of the world's tallest observation wheels.

Mile 25: The tower clock known as Big Ben stands tall and proud next to the Houses of Parliament.

EASTER

For Christians, Easter is one of the most important festivals of the year. It celebrates Jesus Christ's return to life three days after he died on the cross.

Easter is on different dates each year depending on when there's a Full Moon in spring. In 2025, Easter is on 20 April.

The Friday before Easter is called Good Friday. On this day, Christians remember Jesus's suffering on the cross. On Easter Sunday, church services celebrate Jesus's rising from the dead as a sign of hope and new life.

Hot cross buns

Capirotada

Many countries eat a meal of roast lamb for Easter lunch. In the UK, hot cross buns are popular Easter treats, while in Mexico, Capirotada – a dessert made of bread – is eaten.

Eggs are associated with Easter because they are a symbol of new life. The first evidence of decorated eggs was found around 60,000 years ago in Africa, and eggs remain a tradition among African Christians today. Many non-Christians enjoy celebrating Easter and give chocolate eggs as gifts – around 80 million are eaten in the UK each year!

In many cultures, the Easter Bunny hides eggs for children to find on Easter morning. In Switzerland, it's the Easter Cuckoo that brings eggs while in some parts of Germany, children wait for the Easter Fox.

EASTER NESTS

These chocolatey Easter nests have just three ingredients, but they look and taste fantastic!

You'll need

- Mixing bowl
- Medium saucepan
- Small heatproof bowl
- Spoon for mixing
- Teaspoon

- 200 g milk chocolate, broken into small chunks
- 85 g wheat shreds
- 2 bags of mini chocolate eggs (100 g each)
- 12 cupcake cases

What to do

1. In the mixing bowl, crush the wheat shreds into small pieces with your hands.

2. Ask an adult to help you melt the chocolate in a small heatproof bowl placed over a pan of simmering water.

> To melt the chocolate, make sure that the bottom of the bowl doesn't touch the water. Don't let the water get too hot, or the chocolate could burn.

3. Pour the chocolate over the wheat shreds and mix.

4. Spoon the chocolate mixture into 12 cupcake cases. Press the teaspoon into the centre of each to make a 'nest'.

5. Place three mini chocolate eggs in each nest.

6. Chill the nests in the fridge for around two hours until they are firm. You can keep them in the fridge, or in an airtight container if you don't want them to be too hard.

WORLD EARTH DAY

On 22 April, billions of people will celebrate World Earth Day. This global event reminds us that we all have a responsibility to look after our planet.

The first World Earth Day took place in 1970. It was a response to a huge oil spill that killed sea life off the coast of California, in the USA.

Today, more than 190 countries take part in World Earth Day. All sorts of activities take place to raise awareness about pollution, global warming and climate change, with the aim of encouraging people to take care of the planet.

The way we live and the choices we make help to make a difference. What could you do to help the planet today?

ARCTIC ICE PROJECT

Sea ice in the Arctic is rapidly disappearing because of global warming. To help slow down the rate at which it's melting, the Arctic Ice Project, based in California, USA, is studying how tiny pieces of glass can help save sea ice.

Scientists working on this project are researching how covering Arctic sea ice in a thin layer of 'hollow glass microspheres' (HGMs) can help the ice reflect more of the sun's heat and energy.

Scientists believe that if we give sea ice a helping hand to reflect more heat, less of it will melt. In particular, new – or 'young' – sea ice will stand a better chance of survival over the summer months. This could mean that young sea ice will be able to build up more layers, eventually turning into tougher 'multilayer' ice, that could help increase ice cover in areas where it is shrinking rapidly.

There is, however, still a lot of research to be done. Scientists must carefully investigate the effects of the hollow glass microspheres on sea life before the project can fully begin.

May

MONDAY	TUESDAY	WEDNESDAY	THURSDAY
			1
5 Early May Bank Holiday	6	7	8 World Red Cross and Red Crescent Day
12 Flower Moon Vesak*	13	14	15 International Day of Families
19	20 World Bee Day	21 International Tea Day	22
26 Spring Bank Holiday	27	28	29

*Dates may vary by location.

FRIDAY	SATURDAY	SUNDAY
2 International Harry Potter™ Day	3	4 International Firefighters' Day
9	10 Clean Up Your Room Day	11
16	17	18 International Museum Day
23 World Turtle Day	24	25
30	31 UEFA Champions League Men's Final	

NATIONAL WALKING MONTH

May is National Walking Month in the UK. The milder weather makes it the perfect time of year to get out of the house and get walking.

Not only is walking great for your health, but it can also benefit the environment. If you can walk to the shops or school instead of taking the car, you will be helping yourself AND the world around you.

Walking is good for you

Walking keeps you fit and active, builds muscles and improves the health of your heart and lungs.

It can also benefit mental wellbeing. Scientists have found that walking, particularly in nature, can make you feel happier, help you focus, and make it easier to learn new things.

Why not challenge yourself to walk more in May by counting your steps or measuring the distance you walk each day? See if you can increase your distance or steps over the month!

Walking is good for the environment

Every time you walk somewhere instead of
using a car, you make a positive choice
to look after the environment.

Choosing to walk instead
of using the car will...

* Limit pollution caused by
  car emissions
* Reduce noise pollution
* Be safer for wildlife
* Reduce damage to the local
  environment and its surroundings

WALK TO SCHOOL WEEK

Walk to School Week starts in May and is a good
opportunity for you and your family to make the
most of the benefits that come from walking.

Could you find out if your
school is doing anything
for Walk to School Week?
Or, arrange to walk to school
with some friends? Introduce
them to the wonders of
walking while having fun!

VESAK

Vesak, sometimes called Buddha Day, is an important day for Buddhists around the world. It is celebrated by many countries every year in May or June on the day of the Full Moon which, in 2025, falls on 12 May.

Vesak is a celebration of the day that Buddha was born, enlightened and died. It is a day to remember the teachings of Buddha and to think about what it means to be a Buddhist.

Buddha (meaning 'the enlightened one') taught his followers that life is about having a healthy balance, being kind and loving, and being content with what you have.

Enlightenment

Buddhists follow the teachings of Buddha to try to achieve 'enlightenment' – a special understanding of life that is about absolute compassion. Buddhists working towards enlightenment look for the beauty and good in everything and seek to help others.

For Buddhists, the lotus flower is a symbol of purity.

The Buddha's teachings are known as 'dharma'. They include:

generosity

kindness

truthfulness

patience

compassion

wisdom

mindfulness

MAKE A MANDALA

To celebrate Vesak, you could make a mandala. A mandala is a circular symbol that Buddhists believe focuses your spiritual and emotional thoughts. Why not collect leaves and flowers, paint them in different colours, and arrange them in a circular pattern to make your own mandala?

CELEBRATIONS

Buddhists around the world celebrate Vesak in lots of different ways with special traditions such as...

Raising the Buddhist flag

Giving to others

Meditating and praying

Visiting a temple

Cleaning their homes

Decorating their temple and home with lanterns and flowers

MAY'S NIGHT SKY

Look out for these night sky objects in May...

Eta Aquariid meteor shower

Halley's Comet creates this impressive meteor shower. It might be tricky to see in the bright moonlight, so for your best chance to spot this spectacular show, you may need to stay up late – perhaps until after midnight! This year, it's best to see the Eta Aquariids around 6 May.

Flower Moon

May's Full Moon is often called the 'Flower Moon' because many spring flowers can be found in bloom at this time of year. This year, the Flower Moon will be on 12 May.

Arcturus

Look out for the bright summer star Arcturus rising in the east after sunset. It has an orange glow and is found in the constellation of Boötes.

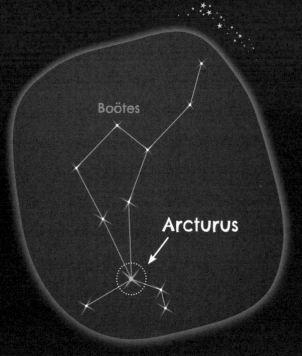

Boötes

Arcturus

The Morning Star

Earth's nearest planet neighbour, Venus, is visible throughout May in the morning sky before sunrise in the east. When it is visible before dawn, it takes on the nickname 'the Morning Star'. At other times, Venus seems to follow the Sun in the west after sunset. At this time, it is called 'the Evening Star'.

Venus is so bright that you can see it during the day! To view it, try looking through a long cardboard tube (like a kitchen towel tube), which can help block out the distracting blue light from the rest of the sky. Be careful not to look directly at the Sun. When you find Venus, it will look like a bright, white point of light.

65

WORLD BEE DAY

Every year, 20 May is World Bee Day. It celebrates the importance of bees, but also helps make people aware of the dangers they face.

Spot some bees! The two most common types of bee you might see are:

Honey bee

Bumble bee

Both types of bees help pollinate plants, but only honey bees make honey. Bumble bee nests can be home to up to 400 worker bees, but honey bees can live in huge colonies of up to 80,000!

Bees can see purple more clearly than other colours, so purple flowers attract bees. Bees – especially long-tongued garden bumble bees – also love tube-shaped flowers.

Buddleia

Catmint

Snapdragon

Lavender

Penstemons

MAKE A BEE HOTEL

Making a bee hotel isn't complicated! Bees love to nest in tubes, so by putting a collection of tubes somewhere in your outdoor space, you might be able to encourage bees to live nearby and pollinate plants in your area!

You'll need

- Hollow tubes
- String
- Container

What to do

1. Group together all your hollow tubes.

2. Once you've gathered the tubes, tie them together with some string.

3. Find a container for them. You can get a grown-up to help you make a purpose-built wooden house for this, or you could use an old mug or plant pot.

UEFA CHAMPIONS LEAGUE FINAL

Football is the most popular sports in the world today and nearly every nation has its own team.

It is a very competitive sport with matches played at many different levels (also known as divisions), from local teams competing at the weekend, to top divisions playing in annual tournaments around the world.

Did you know?
The only country in the world that does not have an official football team is the Marshall Islands.

THE TRUCE

During World War I, on Christmas Day in 1914, English and German soldiers were said to have held a truce (an agreement to stop fighting). They met in 'no man's land', exchanged gifts, took photographs, and played football together.

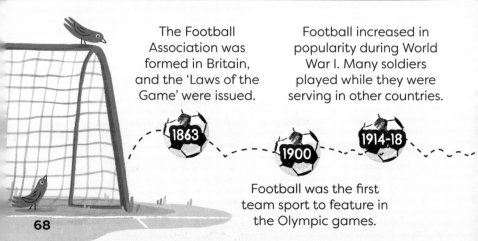

The Football Association was formed in Britain, and the 'Laws of the Game' were issued.

Football increased in popularity during World War I. Many soldiers played while they were serving in other countries.

1863

1900

1914-18

Football was the first team sport to feature in the Olympic games.

2024-2025 LEAGUE

The UEFA Champions League is an annual football tournament often referred to as 'the world's greatest club competition'. Top-division clubs from around Europe all compete for the title.

2024-2025 marks the 70th season of the tournament and is the first to be played under the 'Swiss System', one of the biggest changes to the Champions League in over 20 years.

This means that instead of being placed into groups of four, all 36 teams will compete as one league. Different rounds of the tournament are played throughout the year, with just two teams reaching the final. The final match will be held at the Allianz Arena in Germany on 31 May 2025.

Who do you think will win the Champions League this year? Real Madrid has had lots of wins in the past, but will 2025 be time for a change?

The first FIFA football World Cup was held in Uruguay. Only 13 teams competed, and Uruguay won.

The first official women's World Cup occurred in China.

1930

1955

1991

2022

The European Cup was founded, later becoming the UEFA Champions League.

England's women's team won the European Championships for the first time.

June

MONDAY	TUESDAY	WEDNESDAY	THURSDAY
2	3 World Bicycle Day	4 Global Running Day	5 World Environment Day
9	10	11	12
16	17	18 International Picnic Day	19
23 International Women in Engineering Day	24	25	26
30 Wimbledon starts			

70

FRIDAY	SATURDAY	SUNDAY
		1 World Reef Awareness Day
6	7	8 World Oceans Day
13	14 World Blood Donor Day	15 Father's Day
20	21 Summer Solstice	22
27 International Pineapple Day	28	29

MINIBEASTS

In June, gardens and parks will be a hive of activity for insects and minibeasts. The milder weather means that bugs of all shapes and sizes are busy building homes, finding food and raising babies.

A minibeast is a creature without a backbone or spine. Creatures without a backbone are known as 'invertebrates'. Instead of having a backbone, minibeasts have other things like shells or exoskeletons (a thin but strong layer on the outside of their bodies), which help support and protect them from harm.

All insects have six legs, and many have wings. Some minibeasts live on land, some take to the air, and others live in the water.

Here are some common types...

Ladybirds & beetles

Bees

Dragonflies

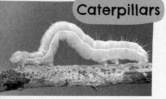

Caterpillars

Butterflies

Ants

Arachnids like spiders have eight legs and two main body parts.

Molluscs have no legs, soft bodies, and some grow shells.

Annelids have soft bodies that are divided into segments like rings.

Myriapods have many pairs of legs.

MINIBEAST SAFARI

Grab a magnifying glass and binoculars and head out to your garden or local park this month to see what fascinating creatures you can find.

Draw a picture of the creatures you find and make a note of where you found them.

After your safari, why not paint small rocks and stones to look like the minibeasts you found and place them around your garden or park to remind you where they all live.

Remember, if you turn over rocks or logs to find minibeasts, be sure to put them back!

WORLD REEF AWARENESS DAY

World Reef Awareness Day began in 2021 and is held on 1 June every year. It is designed to raise awareness of the threats to the world's coral reefs.

Organisers hope that it will help businesses and communities understand how their actions affect the seas and oceans and the impact they can have on the fragile reefs within them.

What is a reef?

Coral reefs are large, colourful structures that develop in warm, shallow ocean waters, often near the equator (the imaginary line around the middle of the Earth). While reefs might look like colourful rocks, they are actually made up of millions of tiny animals called coral polyps, which are supported by plants and algae. Corals produce calcium carbonate, which builds up over time and forms impressive underwater structures. Coral reefs grow and change over thousands of years. The first reefs were formed over 200 million years ago, and most of today's reefs are between 5,000 and 10,000 years old.

Coral reefs provide food and shelter for many different sea creatures, like fish, sea turtles, starfish and even sharks.

The world's largest coral reef is the Great Barrier Reef in Australia. It is so big that it can be seen from space!

What is happening to the reefs?

Scientists have noticed that many reefs have been damaged by bad fishing techniques and people swimming down to touch – or even take – bits of coral. Sewage, plastic and chemical pollution in the oceans also cause damage to the reefs.

Global warming is one of the biggest threats to coral reefs. Coral gets its beautiful colours from the algae that lives inside. When the surrounding water becomes too warm due to global warming, the coral gets rid of the algae and turns white. This is called bleaching, and shows that the reef is in danger.

Get involved!

* Use a reusable water bottle to reduce plastic waste.
* Make a poster to help spread awareness.
* Use reef-safe sunscreen.
* Join a beach clean.

INTERNATIONAL PICNIC DAY

The summer months offer the perfect opportunity for picnicking.

Picnics became popular in France after the French Revolution in 1799. The revolution was a time of fighting and civil unrest in France. After the revolution ended, Royal Parks were opened to the public for the first time, and people began enjoying picnics in the beautiful surroundings of these parks. Soon after, the popularity of picnics spread across Europe and around the world.

International Picnic Day is celebrated on 18 June. It is a time to gather with friends and family and enjoy delicious food outdoors.

Getting involved with International Picnic Day is easy! Find out if there is an event being held near you, or plan a picnic of your own in a local park and invite friends and family. If you prefer a quieter picnic, why not have one in your garden?

PERFECT PICNIC

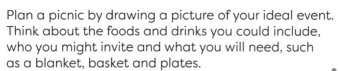

Traditional picnic foods include pies, sandwiches, sausage rolls, cheese, fruits and cakes, but you can choose any foods you really enjoy. Make sure it's something you can eat sitting on the ground, though – something like spaghetti bolognese will be quite tricky!

Plan a picnic by drawing a picture of your ideal event. Think about the foods and drinks you could include, who you might invite and what you will need, such as a blanket, basket and plates.

You could even make a dessert using fruits you have grown or picked yourself, like strawberries (see page 47 for how to grow your own). Eton Mess is great for a summer picnic and will make use of any kind of strawberries – home-grown or shop-bought!

ETON MESS

You'll need

- 200 g strawberries
- 100 ml double cream
- 2 meringue nests
- 2 tbsp icing sugar

What to do

1. Chop up the strawberries into bite-size pieces.

2. Crush the meringue nests into chunks.

3. Whip up the double cream with the icing sugar.

4. Stir the strawberries and meringue into the cream and serve.

SUMMER TIME

When summer begins to arrive, you may hear people saying that the days are getting longer. Is this true? Are the days actually getting longer?

During the summer, the days seem longer because there are more hours of sunlight and fewer hours of night-time darkness. This happens because of the way the Earth travels around the Sun and rotates around its tilted axis (the imaginary line that joins the north and south poles).

In the Northern Hemisphere, summer happens when the Earth's North Pole is tilted towards the Sun. This means that countries in the Northern Hemisphere, like the UK and North America, get more hours of daylight.

When the Northern Hemisphere experiences summer, the Southern Hemisphere experiences winter, and vice versa.

SUMMER SOLSTICE

When the North Pole is at its closest to the Sun, we get the longest day of the year – the day with most hours of sunshine. This is known as the summer solstice, which is the official first day of summer. In 2025, the summer solstice falls on 21 June.

Celebrate summer solstice

For thousands of years, people worldwide have celebrated the summer solstice as the return of the light and life. It has also been a time to come together to bring hope for a good harvest for the rest of the year.

The solstice is often marked by gathering with friends and family, and celebrating with music, singing, dancing, tasty food, bonfires and craft activities.

Why not make a suncatcher?

Stonehenge

Stonehenge is a famous prehistoric stone monument in the south of England. During the solstice, the Sun rises through the middle of the stones. This only ever happens during the solstice, so people from all over the world gather at Stonehenge on this special day to celebrate summer.

WIMBLEDON

Wimbledon (also called 'The Championships') is the oldest tennis tournament in the world. The first tournament was played in 1877.

Every year, the best players from around the world compete in this two-week-long tournament, which starts at the end of June in 2025. The men's and women's finals are played two weeks later on the famous Centre Court at the All England Lawn Tennis and Croquet Club in Wimbledon, London.

Wimbledon is one of four Grand Slam tournaments in tennis (the others are the Australian Open, French Open and US Open). The world's best players aim to win all four so they can be named the world's Grand Slam Champion.

Tennis is thought to have begun in France in the 11th century when French monks used to play a similar game that involved hitting a ball with the palms of their hands.

Did you know?

It's a tradition to eat strawberries and cream at Wimbledon, and nearly 170,000 portions are served each year!

The rules and equipment used in tennis today were first introduced in England in the 19th century by Major Walter Clopton Wingfield.

THE RULES OF TENNIS

Tennis is played in singles matches (one-on-one) or doubles (two-on-two).

A tennis match is played on a court with halves on either side of a net that are divided by lines. Players use rackets to hit the ball over the net within these lines. Hitting the ball back and forth over the net is known as a rally.

Tennis does not have a set time for a match. Matches are divided into games and sets and last for as long as it takes a player to win. You need 4 points to win a game and 6 games to win a set. Matches continue until a player wins by two sets. Games are won by scoring points, but the way points are scored relies on your opponent making a mistake, such as...

Did you know?
Over 50,000 tennis balls are used every year at Wimbledon.

* Missing a ball that was accurately hit onto their side of the court.
* Letting the ball bounce twice before hitting it back.
* Missing or messing up 2 serves in a row (double faulting).
* Hitting the ball outside of the lines.
* Hitting the ball into the net.

Famous professional tennis players

Novak Djokovic

Ons Jabeur

Jannik Sinner

Coco Gauff

Carlos Alcaraz

Elena Rybakina

81

July

MONDAY	TUESDAY	WEDNESDAY	THURSDAY
	1 International Joke Day	2 Women's Euro Championship begins	3
7 World Chocolate Day	8	9	10
14 World Chimpanzee Day	15	16 World Snake Day	17
21	22 World Brain Day	23	24
28	29 International Tiger Day	30 International Day of Friendship	31

FRIDAY	SATURDAY	SUNDAY
4	5	6
11 World Population Day	12	13
18	19	20 World Chess Day
25	26	27

GO CAMPING

If you want to enjoy the peace and beauty of nature, why not go camping? Gazing up at the stars at night and waking to the birds singing can help make you feel relaxed and happy. A camping trip is also an opportunity to learn skills, such as building fires, pitching a tent and cooking outdoors.

First, pitch your tent...

Choose a flat spot to set up your tent. If you don't have a tent, build a den instead! When your tent or den is ready, make it cosy using airbeds, pillows and blankets to keep you cosy, warm and comfortable.

Next, build a campfire...

Make sure you ask a grown-up to help you learn how to make and safely put out a campfire.

1. Set up a firepit away from trees, tents or anything that could catch fire. Surround it with stones to stop fire spreading.

2. Gather dry wood and tinder (dry twigs, leaves and grass).

3. Place some tinder in the centre of your firepit and add some small pieces of dry wood on top.

4. Light the tinder with a lighter, match, or flint and steel.

5. As the fire catches light, add more bits of tinder and dry wood to help it grow.

Keep a bucket of water nearby to put out the fire. Make sure your fire is fully extinguished once you're done.

ENJOY YOUR CAMP!

Once you have set up camp, you can start having fun. Here are some traditional camping activities.

Toast marshmallows & make s'mores

1. You'll need an adult to help with this. Thread a marshmallow onto a stick.

2. Hold it over the campfire, turning it slowly to gently toast it. Try not to burn it!

3. When your marshmallow is golden, eat it as it is, or place it between two biscuits with a small piece of chocolate to make a s'more.

Sing songs and tell stories

Gather round the campfire to sing your favourite songs or learn a traditional campfire song like 'Campfire's Burning'.

You could make up stories or read some of your favourite books. It can be just as fun camping in your garden or an indoor den if you don't have a garden.

Look at the night sky

Around 4 July, spot Mercury above the horizon in the west, just after sunset.

At the end of July, look for Delta Aquariid meteors coming from the constellation Aquarius. They're created by debris from a comet named 96P/Machholz.

JULY MOON PHASES

2nd   10th   18th   24th

INTERNATIONAL JOKE DAY

How do pandas stay cool in July?
They use bear conditioning.

If you liked that, you're going to *really* enjoy these two pages!

On 1 July, countries worldwide celebrate International Joke Day. This is a great excuse to tell your favourite side-splitters!

Joke telling is not a modern-day invention. Thousands of years ago, before people learned to read and write, jokes were recorded in pictures. The oldest joke in the world was thought to be told in 1900 BCE.

So, get your giggle on, flex your funny bone, and share your favourite rib ticklers with your friends and family this month.

Try inventing your own jokes!

Many jokes are about surprising your audience, so you could start by making them think a certain way but then add a sudden twist that surprises them at the end!

What time is it when a jaguar walks into the room?
Time to get out!

Other jokes rely on puns – so using words with double meanings, or similar spellings or sounds.

What musical instrument is found in the bathroom?
A tuba toothpaste

What does a cloud wear under its raincoat?
Thunderwear

Why was 6 afraid of 7?
Because 7,8,9.

What did the police officer say to their belly button?
You're under a vest.

What kind of music do balloons dislike?
Pop!

Why do bees have sticky hair?
They use a honeycomb.

What do you call a magical dog?
A labracadabrador.

What's worse than finding a bug in your sandwich?
Finding half a bug.

What do you call a bear with no teeth?
A gummy bear.

Why aren't cats very good at dancing?
They have two left feet.

Why did the ocean blush?
Because the seaweed.

How do you make an octopus laugh?
Ten-tickles.

WOMEN'S EUROS

In July, you will hear about the Women's Euros, which is the UEFA European Women's Championships. The tournament is held every four years, with the top 16 European teams competing for the title.

This year will be the 14th edition of the Women's Euros and it will be held in Switzerland between 2 and 27 July. The current champions are England. The most successful team to date is Germany, who have won 8 out of 13 Championships up to 2022.

HISTORY OF WOMEN'S FOOTBALL

Football has been a popular sport for many women for years and they have played an important part in shaping the game throughout history. However, it has only recently received attention on TV and in the news in the same way as men's football.

New rules to ban violence were introduced, which made it more socially acceptable for women to play football.

1863 • • • • • 1881 • • • • • • •

The first recorded women's football match was played between England and Scotland.

Who could be the key players in 2025?

Beth Mead

England

Alexia Putellas

Spain

Lena Oberdorf

Germany

Get involved!

Follow your favourite team's progress by finding out more about their players and watching the matches on TV.

If you enjoy watching the women's Euros and would like to give football a try, you could get involved with your school team, practise football skills in your garden or the park, or find out if your town has its own team you can join.

The FA banned women's games being played on professional grounds.

Women's football was included in the Olympic Games.

1921 ••• **1970** ••• **1996** ••• **2008** •••

The ban on women's football was lifted, and the first women's World Cup tournament was played.

The FA apologised for banning women's football (87 years later!).

WORLD CHOCOLATE DAY

7 July – World Chocolate Day – is a delicious day of the year! It is a day when people from all around the world celebrate this tasty treat.

Nowadays, chocolate is a sweet and creamy delicacy that comes in all the shapes, sizes and colours imaginable, and you can buy it at almost any grocery shop in the world.

However, chocolate hasn't always been the milky, sugary treat that is enjoyed today. Chocolate, or rather the cocoa it is made from, has been eaten by people for thousands of years. Before chocolate was invented, cocoa beans were used to make a bitter drink.

Cocoa beans were so popular that people used to trade them for things they needed – they were used like money.

How is chocolate made?

Chocolate is made from the beans found inside the fruit of cacao trees. The beans are dried and roasted to create cocoa – one of the main ingredients in chocolate.

The cocoa is mixed with other ingredients, like milk and sugar, to create the smooth, melt-in-your-mouth chocolate you can buy today.

GET INVOLVED!

Take part in World Chocolate
Day by making some chocolate bark...

You'll need

- Bars of milk, dark and white chocolate
  (or any combination you like)
- Your favourite toppings, like sweets, chocolate chips,
  dried fruit or biscuits

What to do

1. Melt the different bars of
chocolate in separate bowls.

2. Line a baking tray with baking
paper and pour on the melted
chocolate. Swirl the different
types of chocolate together
in a layer that is 1 cm thick.

3. While the chocolate is still
melted, decorate your bark
with toppings of your choice.

4. Allow the chocolate to cool.

5. Break the bark into smaller
chunks and enjoy!

Ask an adult
to help you melt
the chocolate in
a small heatproof
bowl placed over
a pan of
simmering water.

WORLD BRAIN DAY

Your brain is a remarkable organ which controls almost everything your body does. Just like the other parts of your body, it works well when it is healthy, but it can run into difficulties if something is wrong.

Fantastic facts about your brain

- Signals from neurons in your brain can travel faster than 250 mph, which is faster than a Formula One Car.
- Exercise keeps your brain healthy as well as your body.
- Around 80 % of your brain is made up of water!

On 22 July, people around the world celebrate World Brain Day. It first began in 2014 and is given a different theme each year. World Brain Day aims to raise awareness about brain health and conditions that can affect the brain.

Get involved!

Meditate to relax and focus your brain. You can find plenty of guided meditations online.

BRAIN TEASERS

Have a go at these brain-training games!

Riddles

1. What appears once in a minute, twice in a moment, but never in a thousand years?

2. What has hands and a face but can't wave or smile?

3. What is yours but mainly used by others?

Animal conundrum

You need to get a fox, a chicken and a bag of grain across a river in a boat, but you can only take them one at a time.

If you leave the chicken alone with the fox, the fox will eat the chicken, and if you leave the chicken with the grain, the chicken will eat the grain.

How do you get everything across the river without anything being eaten?

Check your answers on page 160!

Animal anagrams

Unscramble the letters in each bubble to reveal an animal.

d a p n a   **l e n h e t a p**   **o r p a l e d**

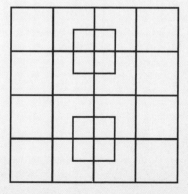

Squares, squares and more squares...

How many squares can you see? If you ask someone else, do they see the same number?

Why not create some of your own riddles and puzzles for friends and family to solve?

93

August

MONDAY	TUESDAY	WEDNESDAY	THURSDAY
4 International Owl Awareness Day	**5**	**6**	**7**
11	**12**	**13** International Wolf Day	**14** World Lizard Day
18	**19** World Orangutan Day	**20** World Mosquito Day	**21**
25 Summer Bank Holiday	**26** International Dog Day	**27**	**28**

FRIDAY	SATURDAY	SUNDAY
1	2	3
8 International Cat Day	9	10 World Lion Day
15	16 International Geocaching Day	17
22	23	24
29	30 International Whale Shark Day	31

ROCK POOLING

August is one of the busiest times for seaside towns across the UK. If you live near the sea or are visiting the beach this month, you might get the opportunity to explore and spot some of the creatures that call the seaside home.

Seaside safari

When the tide goes out, lots of interesting creatures get left behind in the shallow waters, known as rock pools. Looking in these pools is like going on a seaside safari!

When you get near a rock pool, move slowly and try not to cast a shadow over it or the creatures beneath the surface might think you are a predator (an animal that eats other animals) and hide.

If you have one, why not take a magnifying glass with you when you go rock pooling? When you find something you'd like to take a closer look at, you can use your magnifying glass to view it up close.

Common Starfish

Stay safe! Wait until the tide goes out before you explore a rock pool, and make sure you have a grown-up with you at all times.

CURIOUS CREATURES

Many creatures in rock pools along the coast are a type of minibeast – just like the ones you might find in your garden. Which of these creatures can you find on your seaside safari?

Anemones can be different colours like red, brown and green.

Shore Crab

Anemone

Hermit Crab

Goby

Limpets

Sea Urchin

Bladderwrack

Sea Lettuce

This is one type of seaweed but there are lots of different ones.

If you're looking at things in a bucket, only keep one creature in the bucket at a time and always return it to where you found it. Replace anything you move (like rocks or seaweed) when exploring.

SUMMER NIGHT SKY

The Universe and our solar system provide some spectacular displays, and amazingly, scientists can predict when most of these will happen!

They use the way the Earth and other planets orbit (move around) the Sun to predict when certain planets will be visible and when other events will happen. The planets orbit the Sun, and the Earth rotates around its axis like clockwork. This means that scientists can use maths to predict the positions of the planets and stars very accurately.

MERCURY

Mercury is the closest planet to the Sun and the smallest planet in our solar system – it's around the same size as Earth's Moon. Mercury is the fastest planet to orbit the Sun – taking only 88 Earth days.

When to spot it

With clear skies, you should be able to spot Mercury on or around 19 August 2025. It will be visible over the eastern horizon just before sunrise. Mercury appears like a bright star, but it can be tricky to pick out as the sky gets brighter.

AUGUST MOON PHASES

 1st
 9th
 16th
 23rd
 31st

Perseid meteor shower

Perseid meteors are produced by debris from a comet named Swift-Tuttle. This shower has lots of meteors per hour, sometimes more than 70 in dark skies! It was first recorded almost 2,000 years ago and occurs every year between July and August. It is called the Perseid meteor shower because it appears to come from the constellations of Perseus and Cassiopeia.

The Perseid meteor shower happens every year between 17 July and 24 August but will be at its 'peak' (most active and visible) between 12 and 13 August.

WORLD ORANGUTAN DAY

19 August is World Orangutan Day. This is a day that aims to promote the conservation of the orangutan's natural habitat.

Young orangutans stay with their mum until they're seven.

An orangutan has an arm span of around 2 metres.

Orangutans build nests to sleep in. They spend about 90 % of their time in the tree-tops.

They are very clever and can use sticks to collect termites and use leaves as gloves to handle spiky fruit.

Rainforests

The orangutan's natural habitats are the rainforests of Borneo and Sumatra. Over the years, more than 80 % of their home has been lost to palm oil farming, human destruction and deforestation. These majestic animals are also hunted – and either killed or captured – as a part of illegal pet trading. They are sadly in danger of becoming extinct.

Palm oil

The destruction of the rainforest to make way for palm oil plantations is one of the biggest threats to the orangutan.

Palm oil is a type of vegetable oil that comes from the fruit of oil palm trees. It is used in almost everything that comes pre-packaged, including chocolate, toothpaste, pizzas, shampoo and deodorant.

There is nothing wrong with palm oil itself but the problem lies in the way that it is produced. Irresponsible producers of palm oil are destroying large areas of the rainforest in order to farm oil palm trees. This not only destroys the homes of the rainforest animals but contributes to carbon emissions and, therefore, increases global warming.

What can you do?

The WWF (World Wide Fund for Nature) suggests supporting companies that use sustainably made palm oil. Look out for the 'CSPO' label on products that show they use certified sustainable palm oil (CSPO).

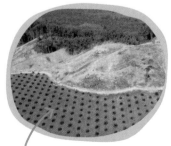

An area of rainforest that has been replaced with a palm oil plantation.

Get involved!

* Visit a local zoo and find out what they are doing to help protect orangutans.
* See if any of your products at home contain palm oil and try to find a CSPO version of each one.

SWIMMING

Swimming is a brilliant way to keep fit and healthy, and it can also be fun splashing about in a pool with friends. Trying to swim a long distance, however, can be quite a challenge!

Open-water swimming has become a popular hobby. This is where people swim outdoors in the sea, lakes and rivers. Open-water swimming is often involved in sporting events like triathlons, but it is also a sport in itself.

People have been dipping in lakes and swimming in the sea for hundreds of years. There are, of course, those who take outdoor swimming to challenging levels and attempt daring feats like swimming the English Channel...

Swimming the Channel

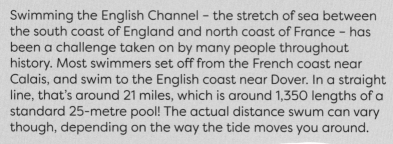

Swimming the English Channel – the stretch of sea between the south coast of England and north coast of France – has been a challenge taken on by many people throughout history. Most swimmers set off from the French coast near Calais, and swim to the English coast near Dover. In a straight line, that's around 21 miles, which is around 1,350 lengths of a standard 25-metre pool! The actual distance swum can vary though, depending on the way the tide moves you around.

Many people who take on this incredible challenge do so to help raise money for charity.

Children's author David Walliams successfully swam the Channel in 2006, raising £1,000,000 for Sport Relief.

150ᵀᴴ ANNIVERSARY

2025 marks the 150-year anniversary of the first person to successfully swim the English Channel without assistance. A British man, Captain Matthew Webb, swam the channel on 24 August 1875.

The swim from Dover, England to Cape Gris-Nes in France took him 21 hours 45 minutes and was the equivalent of swimming 39 miles!

51 years later, on 6 August 1926, an American woman named Gertrude Ederle became the first woman to swim the English Channel. Not only did she swim the Channel, but she also beat the men's record at the time by 2 hours. She swam the equivalent of 35 miles in 14½ hours!

Stay safe

All swimming can be dangerous, but especially open-water swimming. Never go swimming without a grown-up, and don't swim in water you aren't familiar with.

Give it a go!

If you want to give open-water swimming a try, there are plenty of supervised clubs you can get involved with that will teach you how and where you can swim safely.

Did you know?

People who swim the Channel cannot wear wetsuits because they are not allowed to use anything that will assist them. Instead, many swimmers cover their bodies in grease to help keep them warm and to protect their bodies from the salty water.

INTERNATIONAL DOG DAY

August hosts International Dog Day – a day for recognising and celebrating our furry friends – every year on 26 August.

Whether you're a fan of dogs or not, it is hard to deny the connections that dogs share with humans and the many amazing things that they do to help us.

Helpful dogs

Dogs have become part of everyday life in so many ways, from having dogs working in schools to support children's mental health to dogs that help the police and military.

These are just two examples of the amazing jobs that dogs do for people every day!

Guide dogs help guide partially sighted and blind people.

Sniffer dogs help detect illegal items stored in airport luggage.

Extraordinary canine careers

Dogs have been the companions and protectors of humans for thousands of years. Sometimes, a dog does something so extraordinary that they deserve extra recognition...

TOGO THE SLED DOG

In 1925, Alaska was hit with a deadly outbreak of diphtheria. Medicines were available to fight the illness but could not be delivered to the remote region of Nome due to the heavy snow storms.

With the lives of over 10,000 people at risk, locals came up with a plan to collect the medicine from the nearest place they could, which was a staggering 674 miles away! They planned to use teams of sled dogs and their drivers (mushers) to help deliver the medicine across the country.

Seppala (centre) and Togo (far left)

Togo and his handler, Leonhard Seppala, were a well-known and successful sled dog and musher combination. They were included in the mission. Through snow storms and temperatures of -30°C, they completed 264 of the 674 miles, while others covered approximately 30 miles each. Togo was 12 years old when the journey took place, a much older dog than the others, making his achievements very impressive!

Togo has been honoured in many ways, with films being made about his heroic deed, and statues and monuments created in his honour.

After this, Togo retired as a sled dog, and Seppala (with Togo's help!) set up kennels to breed and train sled dogs. Amazingly, it is thought that all modern Siberian Husky breeds can trace their ancestry back to Togo and Seppala's kennels.

SUMMER PUZZLES

Find these words in the wordsearch:

ice cream   flower   camping   sunshine

rock pool   minibeast   strawberry   picnic

r	o	c	k	p	o	o	l	m	a	b	s
b	m	i	n	i	b	e	a	s	t	o	u
i	y	i	c	e	c	r	e	a	m	v	n
n	r	q	u	i	z	e	l	f	c	a	s
f	r	c	x	u	o	k	a	m	l	p	h
p	e	c	i	o	w	g	j	v	r	m	i
f	b	c	y	p	p	e	i	f	o	l	n
l	w	e	a	i	n	o	k	b	c	e	e
o	a	o	i	c	l	l	e	s	p	j	e
w	r	r	e	n	r	i	r	h	a	o	o
e	t	s	e	i	r	e	h	m	a	l	p
r	s	j	s	c	a	m	p	i	n	g	t

Can you solve this riddle?!

I'm surrounded by water, but I'm not a sea creature...

Check your answers on page 160!

What am I?

Help the bee find its way through the maze to the wildflowers.

Rearrange the letters in these word wheels to spell out things you would find at the beach.

s a w v e

c a b r

l h e s l

September

MONDAY	TUESDAY	WEDNESDAY	THURSDAY
1	2 World Coconut Day	3	4
8 International Literacy Day	9	10	11
15	16	17	18 World Bamboo Day
22 Autumn Equinox	23 International Day of Sign Languages	24 World Gorilla Day	25
29 World Heart Day	30 International Podcast Day		

FRIDAY	SATURDAY	SUNDAY
5 International Day of Charity	6	7 National Cinema Day
12	13 Positive Thinking Day	14
19 Talk Like a Pirate Day	20	21 World Gratitude Day
26	27 Women's Rugby World Cup Final	28 World Rivers Day

FORAGING

The autumn months are the perfect time to get out in the fresh air and go foraging. Late August into September is a great time to start.

Foraging is when you go out to find and gather food that grows in the wild. Many people think that foraging is only for people who live in the countryside, but urban areas like towns and cities also have plenty of places to find tasty treats.

Go foraging because...

* It's a fun activity to do with family and friends, in the fresh air.
* You'll find some new foods to taste and you can try new recipes with the foods you forage.
* You will learn where the food you eat comes from.

If you go foraging in September, you are likely to come across a range of fruits, nuts, seeds and vegetables. Here are some common things to forage.

raspberries

strawberries

blackberries

elderberries

mint

chestnuts

crab apples

hazelnuts

Know what you're looking for

Take a field guide to help you identify the plants you come across. Many berries look the same, and some are harmful to humans. You need to know which plants are edible and which might be dangerous. A foraging guide will help you identify the right ones by looking at other parts of the plant, such as the leaves or flowers. Some berries, like blackberries, strawberries and raspberries, can be eaten raw, whereas others, like elderberries, must be cooked.

> **!** **Never eat a berry or plant that you are unsure of and always take a grown-up with you.**

Don't take more than you need

The foods you are foraging for are also a source of food for animals such as birds and squirrels, so never take more than you need. Always leave some for the wild animals as they may be depending on these foods to get through the winter.

Be sure also that you have permission before you start collecting foods – some places are protected and foraging is not allowed.

Ready, steady, bake!

Once you have gathered your natural nibbles, have a go at cooking with them. You could make sweet jams, blackberry crumble, apple pie, roasted hazelnuts and chestnuts, and tangy cordials and teas.

blackberry crumble

SECOND HAND SEPTEMBER

Have you ever considered how much pollution is produced when new clothes are made or where old clothes end up when you no longer wear them?

The charity Oxfam estimates that making a new pair of jeans produces as much pollution as driving a car for over 58 miles! Most old and used clothes and fabric also end up in landfills.

DONATE, REUSE AND RECYCLE

In 2019, Oxfam began promoting Second Hand September. This is a campaign that aims to teach people about the impact the fashion industry has on the environment to encourage them to make fashion choices that are kinder to the environment.

It is hoped that, during September, people will avoid buying new clothes and will instead choose to buy things second-hand. Oxfam aim to encourage more people to start donating, reusing, and recycling older items so that fewer items end up in landfills and fewer new items have to be produced in the future. This helps make fashion more sustainable.

It's easy to buy second-hand clothes – not only on the high street at charity shops, but also on special online stores.

Get involved!

* Go through your wardrobe to see if there are any items you could donate to a friend, family member or charity shop.

* Ask a grown-up to take you to a charity shop for any items you might need, rather than a shop where you would have to buy the item new.

* Look at any clothes you might be thinking of getting rid of and see if you could create something new by giving them a new purpose or by upcycling.

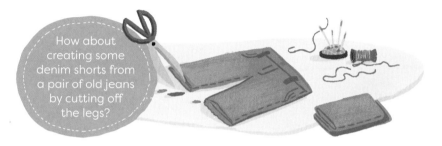

How about creating some denim shorts from a pair of old jeans by cutting off the legs?

EASY UPCYCLING IDEAS

Giving old clothes a new lease of life doesn't have to be tricky!

Try adding some colour to any clothes that have holes in them by sewing on patches.

Make fashionable shopping bags out of old clothes.

Try your hand at tie-dying old plain T-shirts.

Why not try making your very own rag rug out of old clothes?

NATIONAL CINEMA DAY

Grab your popcorn and find a comfy seat – it's National Cinema Day!

National Cinema Day is held on 7 September. Many cinemas across the UK take part in this celebration of cinema and offer discounted tickets to some of the year's favourite blockbusters.

Why have a National Cinema Day?

National Cinema Day was first held in 2022. It aimed to encourage people back to the cinemas after visitor numbers dropped during the COVID-19 pandemic. The day has now become an annual event and promotes visiting the cinema to remind you how impressive the big screen experience can be!

HISTORY OF CINEMA

The earliest surviving film is believed to be *Roundhay Garden Scene*, made in Leeds in 1888. Many people believe that the history of modern cinema and movies began in Paris in 1895 when the Lumière brothers began holding public screenings of their short films. These black and white films were only a few minutes long and had no recorded sound. Colour movies came later, with films like *Gone with the Wind* and *The Wizard of Oz*, both released in 1939.

Since then, the movie experience has developed rapidly, and at most cinemas, you can now enjoy films in 3D. Some cinemas even offer a 4D experience, with special effects like motion, smells, water, wind, fog and flashing lights!

What is your favourite film and which film are you looking forward to seeing this year?

MAKE YOUR OWN MOVIE

Why not have a go at making your own stop-motion film? Stop-motion films are made in a similar way to the original movies. Objects, like a toy, are moved (by you) bit by bit, and photographed after every tiny movement. The images are then joined together and watched back quickly, one after the other, so that the objects look like they're moving! All you need to make one is a smartphone camera and an app. Check with a grown-up before downloading and using apps.

How to get started

1. Set up your starting scene with any character(s) you like. Small, posable figures work best, but you could even try making your character(s) out of soft clay.

2. Take a picture of your starting scene.

3. Make a small change to your scene, like moving a character's arm or leg, then take a photo of the scene again. Keep the camera steady and in the same position as in step 1 for every photo.

4. Repeat step 3, continuing to move and photograph your character(s) until your scene is complete.

5. Ask a grown-up to help you use an app to join your photos together into a movie.

WOMEN'S RUGBY WORLD CUP

The 2025 Women's Rugby Union World Cup will be hosted in the UK. Matches begin in August and the final is expected to be played at Twickenham on Saturday 27 September.

This World Cup will be the 10th edition of the tournament and is being called an 'era-defining tournament' with 16 women's teams from around the world competing for the win in a sport that requires immense speed, strength and skill.

History of women's rugby

The popularity of women's rugby has increased rapidly in recent years, and the sport's professional level is starting to receive a similar level of interest as the men's game. However, at one time, women who wanted to play rugby had to do so in secret as it was frowned upon by society and seen as too brutal for women.

Emily Valentine became the first woman to play rugby officially.

The first ever officially-recorded women's rugby team was formed at Edinburgh University.

1884 • • • • • • • • 1917 • • • • • • • 1962

The first official charity rugby matches featuring female teams were held.

WORLD CUP HISTORY

To date, there have only been three countries that have been triumphant in the World Cup. The United States won the first Women's Rugby World Cup in 1991, England have won the tournament twice, and the most successful country is New Zealand, who have won six out of nine tournaments. New Zealand will be the defending champions after winning in 2021.

Get involved!

* Tune in and watch the tournament. You could make a poster to record the winners of each match and to figure out who will be in the final.
* Research your favourite players.

Who could be the key players in 2025?

Marlie Packer	Gabrielle Vernier	Portia Woodman	Emily Scarratt

England

France

New Zealand

England

The first Women's Five Nations (later becoming the Six Nations) tournament held.

England's players became the first official women's full-time professional rugby players.

| 1991 | 1999 | 2016 | 2019 |

The first Women's Rugby World Cup took place.

Both men's and women's rugby were included in the Olympic Games.

WORLD HEART DAY

Your heart is one of the most impressive organs in your body. It's so good at its job that it is easy to forget about it sometimes!

On 29 September – World Heart Day – people are encouraged to make good choices that will help keep their hearts healthy and beating happily.

Did you know?
Your heart is a muscle that beats all by itself, over 100,000 times a day! Special cells in your heart keep it beating with electricity.

Heart-healthy foods

A healthy heart starts with a healthy, balanced diet. Having a healthy diet doesn't mean cutting out all of your favourite foods – it's about choosing a variety of foods and making sure you include certain things.

Heart-healthy foods include fruit and vegetables; oily fish like salmon, tuna and trout; lean meats like chicken and turkey; eggs; nuts and seeds; beans, lentils and chickpeas; and whole grains like brown rice, oats and wholegrain bread.

Get moving!

Like all muscles, you need to use your heart to keep it strong. This means getting some exercise! Experts recommend around an hour of pulse-raising activity every day.

Why not plan a heart-healthy meal for you and your family? Or host a family fitness challenge? You could see how many jumping jacks, skips or burpees each family member can do in 30 seconds! Who will be the champion?

TOTAL LUNAR ECLIPSE

On 7 September, you may be able to see a
Full Moon **and** a total lunar eclipse. A lunar eclipse
can only happen during a Full Moon.

A lunar eclipse happens when
the Earth is between the
Moon and the Sun, and
the Earth's shadow is
cast onto the Moon.
During the eclipse,
the Moon will
gradually get darker
until the total eclipse
occurs, and at the
peak of the eclipse,
it will appear a
rusty red colour.

Saturn

On 21 September, Saturn will
be as close to Earth as it gets and
will be fully illuminated by the Sun, so keep an eye
out for it! It will shine brightly all night. If you have
a telescope, you might be able to see Saturn's iconic
rings and moons!

Neptune

On 23 September, there will also be the opportunity
to spot the famous blue planet, Neptune, through
binoculars or a telescope. This 'gas giant' will look
like a tiny blue dot in the sky.

SEPTEMBER
MOON
PHASES

7th

14th

21st

29/30th

October

MONDAY	TUESDAY	WEDNESDAY	THURSDAY
		1	2 National Poetry Day
6 World Habitat Day	7	8 World Octopus Day	9
13	14	15	16 World Spine Day
20	21 Diwali	22	23 International Snow Leopard Day
27	28	29	30

FRIDAY	SATURDAY	SUNDAY
3 World Smile Day	4 World Space Week starts	5 World Teachers' Day
10 World Mental Health Day	11	12
17	18	19
24 United Nations Day	25 World Pasta Day	26 National Pumpkin Day
31 Halloween		

BATS

As the nights get longer and darker in October, you may notice some small creatures flitting around just after sunset. If you do, it's likely you will have spotted a common pipistrelle bat.

Go bat spotting!

Most bats are nocturnal, meaning they sleep during the day and come out at night. They live almost all over the UK.

To spot a bat, wait until around 20 minutes after sunset and look for a quiet place with trees and lots of flying insects. When you see them swooping and flitting around, they are probably catching their breakfast!

Many insects are attracted to light, so it's common to see bats flying around gardens and street lights near light sources. Bats navigate and hunt down their prey using echolocation, where they let out a high pitched sound that bounces back off objects around them. The echo that comes back to the bat helps them know how far away their prey is, and what size – and even texture – it is.

Did you know?
Bats are fast fliers, zooming at speeds of up to 100mph!

During October, bats need to catch and eat enough to get them through winter hibernation. Many bats will be in full hibernation by December. When hibernating, they usually choose a warm, safe place like a barn, shed or attic space.

HALLOWEEN

31 October is a time to attend parties, carve pumpkins, and dress up as your favourite spooky character. Vampires, werewolves and witches go out for 'trick or treating', but have you ever thought about why these traditions started?

Halloween is believed to have started over 2,000 years ago. It was originally a religious celebration known as 'All Hallows Eve'. People thought that on the last night of October, the spirits of the dead could return to Earth for one night. People would start bonfires, and leave food and gifts for the spirits to keep them happy. They would also dress up to disguise themselves as spirits so they wouldn't be recognised.

Modern Halloween traditions include picking and carving pumpkins, dressing up and going 'trick or treating'.

Always ask a grown-up to go with you if you're going out 'trick or treating', and only knock on the doors of people you know.

Perfect pumpkins

If you planted pumpkin seeds in April, it could be time to harvest them! If not, pick your own pumpkin at a pumpkin patch or buy one from a supermarket.

There are many creative ways to decorate a pumpkin, from carving to painting. How will you decorate yours?

BOO!!

BLACK HISTORY MONTH

In the UK, October is Black History Month. This is a special time of year to celebrate, commemorate and honour the achievements, struggles and contributions of Black people throughout history.

Black History Month can be traced back to 1926 when Carter G Woodson created a special week to honour and celebrate African American people's contributions to the USA. In later years, in the USA, February became Black History Month. Black History Month was first honoured in the UK in October 1987 and has since become an annual event.

Carter G Woodson

Why is Black History Month important?

Learning about the history of all cultures and societies is important to help us understand them. Throughout history, Black people have often been treated unfairly and very badly. Black History Month gives us the opportunity to learn about, understand and appreciate Black history and culture and to celebrate some of the incredible achievements and contributions Black people have made.

Musicians performing at the Notting Hill Carnival, London – a yearly celebration of Caribbean culture and Caribbean British people's contributions.

Black History Month helps to fight racial discrimination. Racial discrimination, or racism, is when people are treated differently because of their culture or ethnicity.

MAE CAROL JEMISON

Mae Carol Jemison is an incredible Black woman who has always wanted to reach the stars. She is an American doctor, engineer and NASA astronaut!

Mae Carol Jemison was born on 17 October 1956 and raised in Chicago. Growing up, she was always ambitious and hard-working and had a passion for science, space and exploration. She graduated from university with several degrees, including Chemical Engineering, African and African American studies and Medicine.

After university, Mae worked as a doctor in the Peace Corps in Liberia and then went on to work as a family doctor.

In 1987, she applied to NASA's astronaut programme and was selected from thousands of other applicants. She joined NASA as an engineer and astronaut, and on 12 September 1992, she made history when she became the first Black woman to travel into space as a crew member of the space shuttle *Endeavour* while it spent eight days in orbit.

In addition to her incredible careers, Mae has also...

* Authored several books
* Appeared on television in Star Trek Next Generation
* Created a space camp for budding astronauts
* Set up the educational organisation, the Dorothy Jemison Foundation
* Become a professor at Cornell University
* Worked on a project for making human space travel to another star possible

During her space flight, Mae orbited the Earth an incredible 127 times!

NATIONAL POETRY DAY

Poems are a powerful and creative way to tell stories, explore feelings and teach lessons. On the first Thursday of October each year, people across the UK celebrate National Poetry Day. In 2025, this day falls on 2 October.

National Poetry Day is a day to celebrate all the beautiful things that poetry can bring to the world. People are encouraged to write, share and experience the wonders of poetry with friends and family. It was started in 1994 by a small charity called *The Forward Arts Foundation*, and each year, it is given a theme such as *Refuge* (2023), *Truth* (2019) and *Freedom* (2017).

Get involved!

Do you have a favourite poem? Could you share it with a friend? Can you bring a smile to someone's face or share some inspiring words? Perhaps you could even write your own poem! Read on to learn all about haikus – a popular type of poem originating in Japan. Why not see if you can create your own haiku?

WRITE A HAIKU POEM

A traditional haiku is a short poem that captures a moment and its feelings, for example a blooming flower or a fluttering butterfly.

Haikus only have three lines so to write a good one, you need to find just the right words to paint your vivid picture. Try it out and have fun creating your haikus!

AUTUMN
by Daniel Thompson

The first line has 5 syllables – set the scene of your moment.

When you say a word you can hear the syllables, e.g. 'gold-en' has two syllables.

Golden parachutes,

Descending through Autumn skies.

Squirrels gather nuts.

The second line has 7 syllables – expand the idea of the first line.

The last line has 5 syllables – add a change in perspective or a final thought.

Did you know?
The Literacy Trust did a survey in which 66.5 % of children said that writing poetry helped them feel better during the Covid-19 lockdown.

WORLD SPACE WEEK

October hosts World Space Week: the days between 4 and 10 October when people worldwide celebrate the incredible progress made in space research and exploration.

Space Week teaches people about the achievements that have been made in science and space exploration, and those that are still to come. Activities and events are set up by schools, space agencies and aerospace companies to increase awareness and inspire people.

How World Space Week began...

World Space Week was started in 1999 by the United Nations and is held on the same dates every year. The dates of this special week were chosen because they commemorate two important achievements.

4 October 1957: The first human-made satellite, *Sputnik 1,* was launched into orbit.

10 October 1967: A treaty – or agreement – was signed, which meant that any further exploration of the Moon or other planets had to be peaceful. Countries would not be allowed to carry out any military or harmful actions in space.

OCTOBER MOON PHASES

7th   13th   21st   29th

NIGHT SKY

The night sky this October will bring some fascinating astronomical events to spot...

Supermoon

On 7 October, the Moon will be on the opposite side of the Earth to the Sun and will be fully illuminated. Supermoons look bigger and brighter than usual as they are closer to the Earth at this time. This will be the first of three supermoons in 2025.

Orionid meteor shower

The Orionid meteor shower will be visible between 2 October and 7 November but will be at its peak (its most active) on the night of 21 October. The meteors are produced by the comet Halley and will appear to come from the constellation Orion.

Mercury and Mars

On 21 October, Mercury and Mars will appear very close together in the morning sky. This is known as a conjunction.

DIWALI

Diwali takes place between October and November, but the date changes each year – celebrations in 2025 begin on 18 October. Also known as the 'festival of lights', Diwali is one of the most popular festivals in India, celebrated by Hindus, Jains and many Sikh and Buddhist communities.

Order of festivities

Diwali is a joyous and colourful festival celebrated around the world. It is the most important celebration in the Hindu culture and marks the victory of light over darkness and good over evil.

18 Oct People clean their homes and buy small gold items. This is to bring good fortune to their household.

20 Oct Small clay pots called 'diyas' are displayed, and people create, and decorate their homes with, colourful lights, candles and beautiful patterns called 'rangoli'.

21 Oct This is the biggest day of the festival. People gather with family to pray to the goddess Lakshmi. They wear new clothes, prepare delicious feasts and watch fireworks.

22 Oct This is the first day of the new year for those who celebrate. People visit friends and families and give gifts.

23 Oct The final day celebrates the bond between brothers and sisters.

Get involved!

If you want to celebrate Diwali, why not try these activities?

* Make a colourful pot or candle holder – a diya – out of clay
* Make a rangoli
* Make a suncatcher

Flower rangoli

Suncatcher

MAKE A DIYA

You'll need

- Clay (air-dry clay works)
- Paints
- Decorations of your choice
- A tealight candle

What to do

1. Roll a small lump of clay into a ball.

2. Place the ball of clay on a smooth surface and use your thumbs to make a dip in the middle of the clay.

3. Mold the clay into the shape of a small dish.

4. Check that your tealight candle fits into the middle of the dish.

5. Leave your clay pot to dry.

6. Paint and decorate your pot with any paint and decorations you like.

7. Leave to dry.

8. Place your tealight in the middle and enjoy.

Only light a tealight if you're with a grown-up, and never leave a lit candle unattended.

November

MONDAY	TUESDAY	WEDNESDAY	THURSDAY
3	4	5 Guy Fawkes Night	6
10 World Science Day	11 Remembrance Day	12	13 ♥ World Kindness Day
17	18	19	20
24	25 National Tree Week	26 World Sustainable Transport Day	27 Thanksgiving

FRIDAY	SATURDAY	SUNDAY
	1 World Vegan Day	2
7	8	9 British Pudding Day
14	15	16
21	22	23
28	29 International Jaguar Day	30

NOVEMBER

WORLD VEGAN DAY

1 November is World Vegan Day. Celebrated all around the world, it is a day dedicated to raising awareness of what it means to be vegan.

What does being vegan mean?

Being a vegan or living a vegan lifestyle means that you choose not to eat or drink anything that contains products made by animals, or use anything that contains animal products or that has been tested on animals.

There are many different reasons people choose a vegan lifestyle. One of the most common reasons is to protect animals, but many believe that being vegan can have huge benefits for your health and the environment.

Health

A vegan diet means eating a lot of plants and plant-based products, including fruits, vegetables, grains, nuts, seeds, soya products and legumes, like beans and lentils.

These foods contain lots of healthy nutrients, fibre and antioxidants (chemicals that are good for your body). This means that your body will be getting lots of good, health-boosting nutrition, which could improve your overall health.

Look out for the vegan symbol on food items and menus that shows something is vegan.

134

Environment

Producing plant-based foods can be better for the environment...

1. **It requires less land**
   Farming plants takes much less space than farming animals. Scientists believe that if we all changed to a vegan diet, we would need 75 % less land for farming.

2. **It produces fewer emissions**
   Plant-based farming uses fewer processes than animal farming so produces less air pollution and fewer emissions. If everyone in the world went vegan, it's thought that emissions and pollution produced by the food industry would drop by 68 % in just 15 years.

3. **It's better for water supplies**
   Farming plants and making vegan foods uses less water overall than animal farming and also produces less run-off. Run-off is when water containing chemicals from farming enters – and pollutes – lakes, rivers and streams rather than being absorbed into the soil.

GET INVOLVED!

More people are becoming vegan each year, and it is now much easier to find vegan options at your local supermarket. Have a look next time you are in a shop and see if you can find something new to try!

GUY FAWKES NIGHT

Today, Guy Fawkes Night is all about bonfires, fireworks and sparklers, but that's not always been the case...

Bonfire Night or Guy Fawkes Night is celebrated on 5 November. People light bonfires, set off impressive fireworks, use sparklers and munch on toffee apples. It is an exciting evening for many people, but have you ever thought about what you are celebrating?

What is Guy Fawkes Night about?

On 5 November 1605, Guy Fawkes, along with a group of plotters, tried to blow up the Houses of Parliament to kill King James I and his members of parliament. The plotters tried to do this because they disagreed with the king's religious views.

Celebrations mark the fact that the gunpowder plot failed, the King survived, and the plotters were found and arrested. Afterwards, the news of the failed plot spread quickly across the country and people celebrated by lighting bonfires around London and other parts of the country. A year later, in 1606, 5 November was declared a national day of celebration. Once again, people lit bonfires and made Guys to put on top.

Explosive fact!
The plotters intended to use 36 barrels full of gunpowder to blow up Parliament!

CELEBRATE GUY FAWKES NIGHT

It is best to go to an official event as they are very exciting and much safer than having a bonfire at home.

Most organised events will have a bonfire, fireworks, food and entertainment. They will also have strict safety measures to ensure everyone stays safe.

You could also do some arts and crafts, or even make some of your own impressive 'fireworks' at home using this experiment...

EXPLOSIVE EXPERIMENT

You will need

- Whole milk
- Food colouring – multiple colours work well
- A toothpick / cotton bud
- Washing-up liquid
- Bowl

What to do

1. Pour some milk into your bowl (about 2 cm deep).

2. Let the milk get up to room temperature.

3. Gently place small drops of food colouring into your milk, leaving space between the drops.

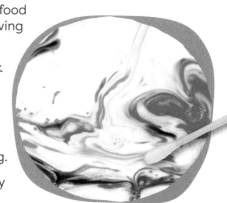

4. Dip the end of the toothpick or cotton bud into some washing-up liquid.

5. Gently dip the soapy end into the milk near to (but not actually in) the colouring.

6. Watch and wait for your very own fireworks display!

WORLD SCIENCE DAY

10 November is World Science Day, or to give it its full title, World Science Day for Peace and Development. It's a day dedicated to science and all the fantastic contributions it makes to the lives of people around the world.

World Science Day was first held in 2002 by UNESCO (United Nations Educational, Scientific and Cultural Organisation) and has since become a yearly event. It encourages more people to consider science as a career and different countries to share scientific knowledge.

Superb science

Science is all around you! It's in the food you eat, the clothes you wear, the technology you use, and so much more.

One of the most significant advances in science recently has been the development of Artificial Intelligence (AI), which scientists and world leaders believe has the potential to change the world for the better.

How could AI change the world?

* Help to create medicines and treatments.
* Make education accessible for everyone.
* Monitor pollution and build a more sustainable future.
* Improve food production.
* Make scientific advancements happen faster.

Can you think of any other ways AI could help make the world a better place?

NIGHT
SKY

You might get lucky enough to spot two meteor showers this month!

Northern Taurid meteor shower

The Northern Taurid meteor shower appears to come from the constellation Taurus and will peak (be at its most active) around 11–12 November.

Leonid meteor shower

This meteor shower appears to come from the constellation Leo. It should be easy to spot as the Moon will not be as bright as it was earlier in the month. This shower will peak on 17 November.

Supermoon

On 5 November, you will get a chance to view the second supermoon of the year. A supermoon looks bigger and brighter than usual because it is closer to the Earth at this time. You might have seen one on 7 October, and there will be another opportunity to spot one on 4 December.

Uranus

On the night of 21 November, you may be able to spot Uranus with binoculars or a telescope. It will appear as a tiny blue-green dot in the night sky.

NOVEMBER MOON PHASES

 5th   12th   20th   28th

NATIONAL TREE WEEK

Have you ever stopped to think about how amazing trees are? Without trees, the world would be a very different place.

The last week in November is National Tree Week – a week for appreciating and recognising the importance of trees.

WHY DO WE HAVE NATIONAL TREE WEEK?

In 1973, people in the UK came together to 'Plant a tree in 73' after thousands of trees died of a fungal disease that spread across the country in the early 1970s. This led to the formation of The Tree Council. In 1975, they held the first National Tree Week to help promote the importance of trees and encourage the care of local woodlands. Trees not only help keep the air clean, but they offer homes to thousands of living things like birds, insects and squirrels, and they help keep soil healthy.

Tree-mendous facts

* Trees clean the air, absorb carbon, produce oxygen and support the atmosphere people need to survive.

  * A single oak tree can be home to over 2,000 different living things.
  * The tallest trees in the world are the Californian Coastal Redwoods, which can grow as tall as ten double-decker buses stacked on top of each other!

Get involved!

Learn about the different types of trees where you live.

Volunteer at a planting day.

Plant a tree in your garden.

Host a tree-growing party.

Plant a tree

You might think that planting and growing is best done in the warmer spring and summer months, but November is actually the perfect time to plant a tree.

1. Choose a place away from other plants so your tree has space and dig a hole the same depth as the roots of your chosen tree.

2. Soak the rootball (the bundle of roots at the bottom of your tree) in a bucket of water.

3. Place your tree in the hole and fill in the gaps around the roots with more soil.

4. Add a tree guard (a sturdy plastic cover to wrap around the trunk) to keep your tree safe.

5. Add a stake (wooden post) to support your tree.

6. Water well.

Terrific trees

Trees not only help the environment, but for some people, simply being around trees helps improve mental wellbeing.

WORLD SUSTAINABLE TRANSPORT DAY

Nowadays, there aren't many places that are more than a car, train or plane ride away. This has lots of advantages such as being able to explore more countries and cultures, but travelling long distances can have some disadvantages too.

Pollution caused by travel damages the environment, so in 2023, the United Nations (UN) decided that 26 November would be World Sustainable Transport Day.

What is sustainable transport?

'Sustainable' means that something can continue to happen without using lots of natural resources and without it having a significant negative impact on the environment.

Sustainable transport means finding ways to keep people travelling while reducing the impact on the environment.

The UN said that sustainable transport should benefit the people of today and the future, be safe, affordable, accessible, efficient and resilient, and have minimum impact on the environment.

Public transport, cycling, walking and car sharing are all examples of sustainable travel.

THE FUTURE OF TRANSPORT

Transportation and technology companies are already working on more sustainable transport methods, such as self-driving vehicles and electric vehicles.

Many believe that the future of transport will include...

* Self-driving vehicles
* Underground roads
* Flying taxis
* Hyperloop

A hyperloop is a shuttle that travels along magnetic rails in tubes with little or no air and could even be solar-powered!

Get involved!

Can you think of a more sustainable way to make your regular journeys, such as cycling to school, walking to the shops or taking the bus to football training?

Design your own sustainable transport

Draw and label your idea. It could be the future of sustainable transport!

* What could it run on?
* Would it transport people or goods?
* Could it be made from sustainable materials?
* How will you make it safe?
* Where would it transport people?

WINTER PUZZLES

Rearrange the letters to unscramble the types of winter clothing.

| c | f | r | a | s |

| | | | | |

| e | k | j | t | a | c |

| | | | | | |

| s | e | l | v | g | o |

| | | | | | |

| s | l | i | w | e | l | e |

| | | | | | | |

| o | l | w | o | y | l | h | t | a |

| | | | | | | | | |

Now rearrange the shaded letters from your answers above to find something you might light to keep warm...

| | | | | | | | |

Fit these animals into the grid below.

Arctic hare   fox   barn owl   grey seal   penguin   robin
snow leopard   polar bear   hedgehog   reindeer

r

r

a

o

Check your
answers on
page 160!

e

Can you solve
this riddle?!

December, January
and February...

**What do they all
have in common?**

December

MONDAY	TUESDAY	WEDNESDAY	THURSDAY
1	2	3	4 International Cheetah Day
8	9 International Day for Veterinary Medicine	10 Nobel Prize Day	11 International Mountain Day
15	16	17	18
22	23	24 Christmas Eve	25 Christmas Day
29	30	31 New Year's Eve	

FRIDAY	SATURDAY	SUNDAY
5 International Volunteer Day	6	7
12	13	14 Hanukkah begins
19	20	21 Winter Solstice
26 Boxing Day	27	28

WINTER WILDLIFE

December, with its bare trees and icy puddles, can seem like a quiet time for nature. But there's still plenty of wonderful wildlife to spot in the countryside, along the coast or in your garden.

Foxes survive the cold by growing a thick winter coat.

Barn owls fly low across fields in search of mice to eat.

Flocks of wild geese fly over marshy areas and wetlands.

Grey seals give birth to furry white pups on remote beaches.

You can find tips for helping garden birds on pages 12–13, and here are some ways in which you can help other wildlife during the cold winter months...

* A frozen pond can cause problems for frogs hibernating at the bottom. Never smash the ice — instead fill a saucepan with hot water and leave it on the ice to melt a hole.

* Always make sure there is fresh drinking water and put out food for hungry visitors. Badgers enjoy cheese, unsalted peanuts and fruit, while squirrels are fond of nuts such as walnuts and almonds.

* Leave piles of leaves and logs alone so you don't disturb hibernating hedgehogs or toads.

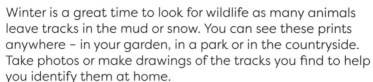

WHO GOES THERE?

Winter is a great time to look for wildlife as many animals leave tracks in the mud or snow. You can see these prints anywhere – in your garden, in a park or in the countryside. Take photos or make drawings of the tracks you find to help you identify them at home.

As well as footprints, look out for other signs of animal activity, including poo, fur and feathers, and nests and dens.

Badgers come out at night, so you won't spot these creatures during the day. They have five toes and long claws, and their tracks are around 11 cm long and up to 6.5 cm wide.

Rabbits' front feet are around 3.5 cm long and 2.5 cm wide, and their back feet can be more than twice as long. You'll often see the prints of two small front feet side by side, followed by their much bigger back feet one in front of the other.

Foxes have four toes, with a triangular-shaped pad at the back. Their tracks are around 5 cm long, and 4 cm wide. Dog tracks can look very similar, but a fox's toes are closer together. Unlike dogs, a fox usually moves in a straight line.

The hooves of deer leave two long marks with a gap in between. The size of the tracks depends on the species, but they all look similar.

Otters leave large, webbed tracks along the waterside – up to 9 cm long, and 6 cm wide. They have five toes, but don't usually leave claw marks. Sometimes, you can see the mark of an otter's dragging tail.

INTERNATIONAL MOUNTAIN DAY

Mountains may be beautiful to look at, but they're important for many other reasons too. They provide fresh water for more than half the world's people and are home to many plants and animals.

International Mountain Day is celebrated on 11 December. This yearly event is organised to raise awareness about the importance of mountains to life.

Every continent on Earth has mountains. Most are part of mountain ranges, such as the Andes in South America, or the Alps in Europe.

Climate change is causing mountain glaciers to melt, which affects the flow of fresh water. Human actvities like the cutting down of mountain forests cause harm to animals and plants.

What is the nearest mountain to where you live? How tall is it? Can you find out what animals and plants live there?

THE HIMALAYAS

Mount Everest, the world's highest mountain, is part of a mountain range called the Himalayas. These mountains run across five Asian countries: India, Nepal, Bhutan, China and Pakistan.

The Himalayas began to form about 50 million years ago, but it's still one of the youngest mountain ranges in the world. From west to east, the mountains stretch for 2,500 km.

Did you know?
The Himalayas are still growing, by more than 1 cm a year!

Many amazing creatures are found in the Himalayas, such as the red panda and a beautiful bird called the Himalayan monal. The endangered snow leopard is known as the 'ghost of the mountains' because it lives high in the peaks and is hardly seen.

Snow leopard

Himalayan monal

Red panda

Mount Everest is 8,849 metres tall. At the summit, the temperature can drop to around -40°C and there's much less oxygen in the air than at sea level. Despite these dangers, hundreds of climbers risk their lives climbing the mountain each year.

Did you know?
The Yeti, or Abominable Snowman, is a legendary monster that is said to roam the peaks of Nepal and Tibet. It is described as a huge ape-like figure with white, shaggy fur.

HANUKKAH

The Jewish celebration of Hanukkah is also known as the Festival of Lights. For eight days, families gather to light candles, eat delicious food and exchange gifts.

The date of Hanukkah changes each year because it is based on the Hebrew calendar, which is influenced by the Sun and the Moon. In 2025, it will begin at sunset on 14 December and continue until the evening of 22 December.

Hanukkah comes from a Hebrew word meaning 'to dedicate'. More than 2,000 years ago, the Jews won a battle for religious freedom and lit an oil lamp to celebrate the victory. Although there was only enough oil for one night, the lamp miraculously burned for eight nights.

Traditional food is an important part of Hanukkah. Food fried in oil is a reminder of the burning oil. Latkes are potato pancakes, often served with apple sauce and sour cream. Another favourite is a sugary jam doughnut called sufganiyah.

Sufganiyah

Hannukah is celebrated by lighting a 'hanukkiah' or 'menorah', a kind of lamp that holds nine candles. The tallest candle in the centre, the 'helper', is lit first, along with one of the other candles. On each night of Hanukkah that follows, an additional candle is lit – using the helper candle – until all eight candles are lit on the last night of Hanukkah.

DREIDEL

Hanukkah wouldn't be complete without playing a traditional game called Dreidel! A dreidel is a type of spinning top with Hebrew letters on each of its four sides.

Children often receive a small gift on each of the eight days of Hanukkah. Chocolate coins are popular because they can be used to play Dreidel. See if you can find a dreidel to buy, or you could try making one from clay and writing the Hebrew letters on each side. The Hebrew letters stand for *Nes Gadol Hayah Sham*, which means "A great miracle happened there".

How to play

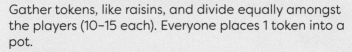

Gather tokens, like raisins, and divide equally amongst the players (10–15 each). Everyone places 1 token into a pot.

Each player spins the dreidel once during their turn. Depending on which side is facing up when the dreidel stops spinning, the player does the following:

נ **Nun** – Nothing.

ג **Gimmel** – Takes the whole pot! Everyone, including the spinner, puts another token in the pot.

ה **Hey** – Takes half of the pieces in the pot (round up to the nearest whole number if there are an odd number).

ש **Shin** – Puts another token into the pot.

Any player that doesn't have any tokens left when landing on a shin, or after another player lands on a gimmel, is out. The game ends when there is one player left.

WINTER SOLSTICE

The winter solstice marks the shortest day and the longest night of the year.

In the northern hemisphere, the winter solstice falls on 21 December in 2025. This is the day when the North Pole is pointed furthest away from the Sun. There will be around seven hours and 50 minutes of daylight in the UK – nine hours less than on the longest day of the year, 21 June!

If it's sunny, go outside and look at your shadow – it will be the longest shadow you cast all year! That's because the Sun will be at its lowest point in the sky.

After the winter solstice, the days start to lengthen again. In ancient times, people built monuments to celebrate the return of the light. One example is Stonehenge, in Wiltshire, England, built around 5,000 years ago. People still gather there to watch the sun rise on the morning of the winter solstice.

The Norse people of northern Europe celebrated the festival of Yule around the winter solstice. Today, some people call the time around Christmas "Yuletide".

In China, the Dongzhi festival celebrates the return of lighter days.

LOOK UP!

Winter is one of the best times to stargaze. On 4 December, there will be a supermoon.

Orion is one of the brightest constellations in the winter sky. To find Orion, look for a row of three stars. These form Orion's Belt Below the belt is a small group of stars, Orion's Sword. Above Orion's Belt, a reddish star called Betelgeuse marks his left shoulder.

Orion
Betelgeuse
Orion's Sword
Orion's Belt
Rigel

Pollux
Castor
Gemini

Keep an eye out for the Geminids meteor shower. In 2025, 14 December will be the best time to look.

The Geminids will appear to come from the constellation Gemini. To find Gemini, look for Orion's Belt. Follow an imaginary line from the star Rigel (Orion's foot), through the belt and the star Betelgeuse. Eventually, you'll reach Gemini's two brightest stars, Castor and Pollux.

CHRISTMAS

As the year draws to a close, many people around the world look forward to Christmas. It's a time for family gatherings, delicious food, exchanging presents and festive cheer.

In most countries, Christmas Day falls on 25 December. For Christians, it's an important religious festival to mark the birth of Jesus Christ. Some attend church services and sing carols.

Christmas is celebrated by millions of non-Christians too. Christmas trees and festive wreaths are popular decorations, and streets and homes are lit up by twinkling lights.

In the UK, people enjoy eating turkey and Christmas pudding, but other countries have their own traditions. Polish people enjoy a beetroot soup called borscht on Christmas Eve, while jollof rice forms part of a popular Christmas Day meal in Ghana.

Borscht

* In the US, children leave Santa treats of milk and cookies on Christmas Eve, while British children might leave out a mince pie.
* In Kenya, children watch out for Santa arriving on his camel!
* In Iceland, it's the 13 Yule Lads who bring gifts. These mischievous trolls leave presents for good children and rotten potatoes for naughty ones!

MAKE A SNOW GLOBE

Enjoy a snowstorm without getting cold! This festive snow globe will make a great Christmas present for someone.

You will need

- Clean jam jar
- Figurine or clay model to fit the jar, e.g. a Christmas tree
- White air-dry clay
- Strong, clear glue
- 2–3 teaspoons of glycerine or baby oil
- 1 teaspoon biodegradable glitter

What to do

1. Mould the clay to make a round base a little smaller than the jar opening. Check that the jar fits snugly around the shape.

2. Follow the pack instructions to dry the clay overnight. When the clay is dry, glue your figurine onto the base. Then glue the base into the centre of the jar lid and leave to dry.

3. Place 2–3 teaspoons of glycerine or baby oil into the jar.

4. Slowly fill the jar with water, leaving a small gap at the top. Then add the glitter and mix.

5. Put a small amount of glue around the rim of the jar. Turn the lid upside-down and gently place your figurine into the water. Screw on the lid and let the glue dry.

6. Slowly turn the jar over to be sure there are no leaks. Then shake up a snowstorm!

INDEX

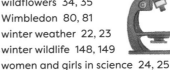

ANSWERS

Page 93

Riddles: 1) The letter 'm' 2) A clock 3) Your name

Animal conundrum: Take the chicken across first, then come back and take the grain across. Take the chicken back, drop it off, collect the fox and take it across to join the grain. Come back for the chicken.

Animal anagrams: panda | elephant | leopard

Squares: There are 40 squares in total.

Pages 106–107

Wordsearch:

r	o	c	k	p	o	o	l	m	a	b	s
b	m	i	n	i	b	e	a	s	t	o	u
i	y	i	c	e	c	r	e	a	m	v	n
n	r	q	u	i	z	e	l	f	c	a	s
f	r	c	x	u	o	k	a	m	l	p	h
p	e	c	i	o	w	g	j	v	r	m	i
f	b	c	y	p	p	e	i	f	o	l	n
l	w	e	a	n	o	k	b	c	e	e	e
o	a	o	i	c	l	l	e	s	p	j	e
w	r	r	e	n	r	i	r	h	a	o	o
e	t	s	e	l	r	e	h	m	a	l	p
r	s	j	s	c	a	m	p	i	n	g	t

Riddle: An island

Pages 144–145

Anagrams:
scarf | jacket | gloves
| wellies | woolly hat

Shaded letters anagram:
log fire

Riddle: The letter 'r'

Maze:

Word wheels: waves | crab | shell

Word grid:

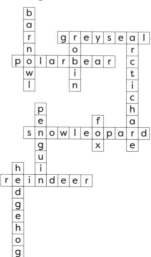